SOUTH TEMPLE STREET
LANDMARKS

Salt Lake City's First Historic District

BIM OLIVER

THE
History
PRESS

Published by The History Press
Charleston, SC
www.historypress.net

First published 2017

Manufactured in the United States

ISBN 9781467137713

Library of Congress Control Number: 2016950695

To Cyndy

CONTENTS

ACKNOWLEDGEMENTS

During the process of researching and writing this book, I often felt that it was a solitary exercise. But it most definitely was not. This book would not have happened without the support and assistance of a number of people.

First and foremost, my thanks to Kirk Huffaker, executive director of the Utah Heritage Foundation, and Barbara Murphy, former director of the Utah State Historic Preservation Office, for encouraging me to explore Utah architecture of the mid-twentieth century, an exploration that led me to South Temple Street of 1925. I was honored that Kent Powell, one of Utah's foremost historians, agreed to review my manuscript. His guidance and insight were invaluable.

I'm grateful to Greg Walz of the Utah History Research Center and Sara Davis of Special Collections at the University of Utah's Marriott Library, who were both patient and persistent in tracking down sometimes obscure images. The staffs at the Salt Lake County Recorder's Office, the Salt Lake City planning department and the Salt Lake County Archives were always gracious and responsive to my requests for information. My thanks, too, to Bill Browning, Burtch Beall and the family of F.C. Stangl for generously sharing their time in personal interviews.

I want to thank the staff at The History Press, especially Candice Lawrence, who made the publishing process as effortless as it could be for a neophyte like me.

There are other individuals and organizations that I'm sure that I've overlooked, but I hope that they can see their contributions in these pages.

"BUILT TO STAND FOR ALL TIME"

In the spring of 1922, when workers completed demolition of the Gardo House at 70 East South Temple Street, they were likely oblivious to the broader implications of their labors. In addition to dropping the mansion's timbers, however, they were also figuratively dropping a curtain on Salt Lake's gilded age. A singular icon of a period known for its icons, the Gardo House had stood on the corner of South Temple and State Streets for a mere fifty years before falling.

Exuberant in its Second Empire frills, "it was said to be the finest... private residence west of Chicago." Not surprisingly, its transience came as a surprise to the community. One elderly resident observing the demolition remarked that when the mansion was constructed, "we all believed that it was built to stand for many years; in fact for all time."[1]

In all its grandeur at the time of its demolition, the Gardo House was not the largest or even the most ornate home in the city. That title would likely have belonged to one of a number of other mansions along South Temple Street. Their presence bestowed an almost mythical character on east South Temple. Named "Brigham Street" in honor of Brigham Young, it was the home of Utah's rich and famous in the early 1900s, a haven of luxurious estates, lavish parties and extravagant lifestyles. According to historian Margaret Lester, "[I]t became the most beautiful thoroughfare between Denver and San Francisco."[2]

But amid the luxurious estates, lavish parties and extravagant lifestyles, change was encroaching on Brigham Street. By the mid-1920s, the party

Built by Brigham Young, the Gardo House stood for fifty years as a symbol of South Temple's affluence and opulence. *Utah State Historical Society.*

would be over. Attrition, economics and changing social mores would conspire to set the stage for a sweeping transformation. By 1925, as the dust settled on the Gardo House site, the engine of change was churning inexorably along the entire length of South Temple.

If South Temple were thought in 1925 to have a singular identity—that of Brigham Street—then the next fifty years would erase that misconception. The changes that would come to South Temple in the middle of the century would be so vast that most of the street would become unrecognizable to the gentleman observing the demolition of the Gardo House. And they would come at great expense to many cherished places along the street that Salt Lake residents assumed would last forever. So much so that by 1975, much of South Temple would be designated by Salt Lake City as a historic district with special protections that would significantly limit the way in which the street evolved from then on. This history, then, is framed by those two years—1925 and 1975—as the beginning and end of the period of greatest change in the places of South Temple.

South Temple's preeminence dated from the earliest days of Mormon settlement. Running past Temple Square, it was given "a stature of importance as the major east–west axis," serving as "the only primary east–

west route in early settlement days between the city and Red Butte Canyon, and Fort Douglas" and as a parade route for community celebrations.[3] That stature grew as South Temple attracted Utah's richest and most influential citizens as residents, and it became a street that exuded wealth and power. Over time, it also became a bustling thoroughfare between Salt Lake's major centers of activity: downtown and the University of Utah. And it was one of just a few streets that connected Salt Lake's commercial center with its industrial and transportation district.

South Temple's significance derived from its unique setting as well. As it travels from the Union Pacific (UP) Depot in the west to Reservoir Park in the east, it runs up a gradual incline. Along its eastern half, South Temple cuts across the base of a steep hill, a topographic distinction that became more pronounced as the city was platted. South Temple came to form "the boundary between two neighborhoods where two different street grids meet."[4] To the north of South Temple sat the Avenues with small blocks and lots crowding the steep hillside. To the south, as the terrain leveled, the city spread out in regular large blocks.

This singular setting—akin to a topographic podium—combined with its role as an increasingly important thoroughfare in the rapidly growing city, gave much of South Temple a prestige unmatched by any other street. Even though its identity was, for many years, almost inextricably associated with that of Brigham Street, South Temple was never a single place. It was really a series of places with disparate personalities that ran the gamut—from dignified and aristocratic to proletarian, even hardscrabble.

Nestled against the University of Utah—from 1300 East to 800 East—the "Upper East" was quiet and reserved. Its residents were, like the late nineteenth- and early twentieth-century mansion builders just down the street, wealthy and influential. But they were not as wealthy and, for the most part, not as influential—and not nearly as ostentatious in their lifestyles. Their homes were certainly large and comfortable but not grand and opulent like the mansions just to the west. While the rest of South Temple would change dramatically between 1925 and 1975, the Upper East would—quietly and reservedly—stay very much the same.

The "Mansion District"—from 800 East to 500 East—carried the air of affluence. Early on, that character was associated with individuals, men and women with instantaneous fortunes and the desire to flaunt their wealth. Flaunt they did, building elaborate mansions, symbols of conspicuous consumption. As the century progressed, however, the Mansion District transformed into a place associated instead with corporate fortune, as companies moved in to take advantage of South Temple's ample space and lingering prestige.

Wedged between the Mansion District and downtown, the "Lower East" spent the years between 1925 and 1975 trying desperately to sort through its many identities. To put it simply, it was confused, disorganized, a jumble of shops and offices and apartments and clubs and churches awkwardly coexisting along the four blocks from 500 East to State Street.

The "Church Blocks" at the north end of downtown, framed on the north by Temple Square and "Administrative Square" and on the south by the city's business center, were staid and businesslike, although they would eventually incorporate a corporate flair. These two blocks between State Street and West Temple were the epicenter of the Church of Jesus Christ of Latter-day Saints' (LDS) domain, and their character reflected the two personalities—nonsecular and secular—of the church itself. The respective progressions of the Church Blocks' north and south sides reflected the LDS Church's need to project an identity that was, at once, both traditional (in its religious activities) and progressive (in its commercial activities).

From West Temple to 400 West, South Temple continued into the "West End," as unruly and disheveled as the Church Blocks next door were calm and ordered. Here South Temple wandered into terra incognita, a lost place without an identity, beyond the awareness of much of the community. If Brigham Street were Salt Lake's golden child, then the West End would be the wayward one, destined to find itself increasingly isolated as the century progressed.

Between 1925 and 1975, South Temple—from the Union Pacific Depot on the west to Reservoir Park on the east—saw as much or more change than any other street in Salt Lake City. Through Salt Lake City's first 125 years, the places of South Temple were works in progress—never quite finished, never quite complete. Between 1925 and 1975 alone, 60 percent of the properties between 400 West and 1300 East experienced significant change—new buildings, demolitions, major remodels and so forth. Many changed more than once.

This history describes the changes along South Temple during those transformative fifty years, from the time when South Temple's persona as Brigham Street seemed destined to last "for all time" to the time when new protective ordinances would dramatically affect the nature of change along much of the street. How South Temple changed qualitatively between 1925 and 1975 is, of course, a matter of opinion. The purpose of this narrative, however, is not to judge how the street has altered but simply to document that transformation with the goal of increasing our understanding of how and why places change.

1

THE WEST END

"A Mixed-Indeterminate Area"

For many Salt Lake residents, it may seem that South Temple Street ends at West Temple Street—that what extends west to the Union Pacific Depot is another street entirely. It's a perception that's justified. From the earliest days of settlement, this three-block stretch from West Temple to 400 West (the "West End") was effectively isolated from the rest of South Temple—and from the rest of the city. Over the years, various community planning initiatives have approached the West End with the goal of saving it from itself but not necessarily of incorporating it into the greater community. When the South Temple Historic District was designated in the mid-1970s, these three blocks didn't even qualify for inclusion; the historic district ended at State Street, two blocks to the east.

In hindsight, the isolation of South Temple's West End seems almost inevitable. But it's contrary to a much more likely scenario, one in which the West End became a commercial hub for the city. Temple Square was originally designated as the geographic center of Salt Lake, with the anticipation that the city would grow around it—in all directions. South Temple was considered the new community's most important street, and its west end was just as potentially significant as the rest of it.

The construction in 1909 of the grand Oregon Short Line Depot (that would become the Union Pacific Depot) would seem to have validated the West End's significance as a natural gateway to the community, as a busy corridor of commercial activity with the railroad station at one end and downtown at the other. The depot was a short three blocks from Temple

Looking west along South Temple from West Temple, circa 1912. *Utah State Historical Society.*

Square and the city's central business district. But development along this stretch of South Temple evolved in a fragmented and incoherent fashion, with a smattering of small commercial businesses, light industrial operations and transient boardinghouses.

As Salt Lake expanded and urbanized, the West End became increasingly isolated—geographically, functionally and socially. Rather than growing and thriving with the rest of the city, it experienced a kind of atrophy, as activity diminished and buildings went vacant and/or were demolished. Behind this "devolution" is a significant question: Why? Why would these blocks seemingly primed for commercial development languish? Why wouldn't the west end of South Temple attain the same commercial and civic significance as Main Street or State Street or even West Temple? What factors caused it to become so isolated?

Early on, west South Temple represented a natural commercial center. The Oregon Short Line/Union Pacific Depot served as a potential western "anchor" for the commercial district that stretched several blocks east to Temple Square and downtown. At the depot, thousands of passengers disembarked and tons of freight were unloaded every month. And since much of the commercial expansion in Salt Lake was driven by Gentile (non-Mormon) interests, it would have seemed natural for those interests to look to the West End as their business center. The railroad, after all, was essentially a Gentile industry, so commercial development should have proceeded apace. But it didn't.

The reason is found in an event that occurred before the turn of the twentieth century: the construction of the City and County Building. The decision in the 1890s to locate it at 400 South in "Emigration Square," well south of the center of Mormon power at Temple Square, was a clear victory for Salt Lake's Gentile political interests. As a result, the City and County Building's location also established a certain center of gravity for Gentile business interests, prompting Samuel Newhouse, one of Salt Lake's most powerful Gentile businessmen, to develop Exchange Place—his "Wall Street of the West"—just across the street from the new center of city government. With Gentile interests occupying its south half and Mormon interests the north half (near Temple Square), Main Street became the focus of an intensifying conflict to establish broader control over Salt Lake's rapidly growing economy.

The competition for control of Main Street—for control of the city's emerging commercial center—left west South Temple out in the cold. With financial and political attention elsewhere, its properties weren't perceived as valuable assets. As a potential commercial center, it was an afterthought. Even after Mormon and Gentile leaders had reconciled in the early 1900s, the West End lay neglected. So it languished. By the 1940s, the disparity in value between Main Street and the west end of South Temple was extreme. "The center commercial district," observed a 1943 city plan, "is quite concentrated along State and Main Streets from South Temple to 5th South Street. Here, land values are extremely high, ranging from $5,000 to $6,000 per front foot, but dropping off very suddenly on adjacent block frontages to $100.00 to $200.00 per front foot and lower."[5]

But the West End's perceived lack of value derived from its own inherent limitations as well. Primary among these, ironically, was the Union Pacific Depot. While the depot generated substantial activity in passengers and commodities, it also created an obstruction to through traffic. South Temple dead-ended at the depot. The result was that access to the West End was limited. The only traffic would have been generated by people who were going there specifically. There was no ancillary traffic, no pass-through traffic, meaning that businesses along west South Temple would have significantly less visibility than their counterparts on through streets (e.g., Main Street). In an era with limited advertising, a business's success might well depend on its exposure. Fewer people meant less exposure to potential customers. Less exposure meant diminished attraction for businesses. Diminished attraction meant depressed property values.

Basic demographics, too, played a role. In the first half of the twentieth century, Salt Lake City was growing rapidly, increasing nearly 60 percent between 1920 and 1950 alone. Home construction boomed—everywhere, that is, except on the west side of Salt Lake City. Population growth in Salt Lake City moved east and south. To the west, the developed city ended essentially at the state fairgrounds—a mere four blocks from the UP Depot—just as it had when the city was originally platted. After World War II, population growth shifted increasingly out to the valley and into adjacent counties, even farther away from west South Temple. These burgeoning communities—Sandy, Bountiful, Orem, et al.—would develop their own commercial centers, further diminishing the West End's already low development values.

Had there been a vibrant residential community on Salt Lake's west side, west of the fairgrounds, it's possible that the West End might have evolved differently. But a relatively small residential population and little commercial activity meant that "city services were extended to the Westside much slower than to other parts of the city."[6] With no resident or business community of its own and with the city's population expanding in essentially the opposite direction, the northwest part of Salt Lake City—including west South Temple—became disconnected from the rest of the community.

These various factors caused the West End to develop in a haphazard fashion. Vacant lots were common. Commercial buildings were small and nondescript, except those constructed as warehouses or small factories. With rare exception, none of the buildings in the West End was taller than two stories. Many housed apartments or boarding rooms in their upper floors. With names like Ignato, Moskowitz and Kaleel, business owners were not members of the city's established political and commercial power structures. West End businesses—Yokohama Tailors, Sarroa Cirilo Pool Hall and Erindira Imported Goods, to name a few—would have attracted only a limited base of customers, primarily from the ethnic communities that had tended to settle west of downtown or from workers associated with the railroads.

Vacant and underutilized properties proliferated. From 1925 to 1960, the number of occupied addresses dropped from 109 to 79. Even where properties were occupied, the intensity of use was diminishing. By 1945, for

Western Salvage was typical of the businesses that populated the West End, the kind usually located in a community's fringe areas. *Utah State Historical Society.*

example, three of the four corners in the block between 100 West and 200 West (now 200 West and 300 West) were occupied by service stations, and the largest businesses were a laboratory supply manufacturer, a creamery, a salvage yard and an electric supply company—the kinds of businesses generally relegated to a community's fringe areas.

By the time that Salt Lake's first general plan was produced in 1943, the West End had degenerated into a lost place. Community perceptions were characterized as, at best, ambivalence. The 1943 City Plan described the area as a "narrow, less desirable, apartment house strip [that] serves as a transition between the main business district and the railroad and industrial area on the west."[7]

Nevertheless, the community seemed to feel a need to do *something* in the West End, so the plan envisioned a grand development at the Union Pacific Depot, with an intermodal transportation center bordered by "Station Park," an open space of grass and trees. Although Station Park didn't materialize, the optimism behind it didn't disappear. Even as late as 1967, the unlikely partnership of the Ford Motor Company and United Airlines proposed to city leaders a study to assess the possibility of creating

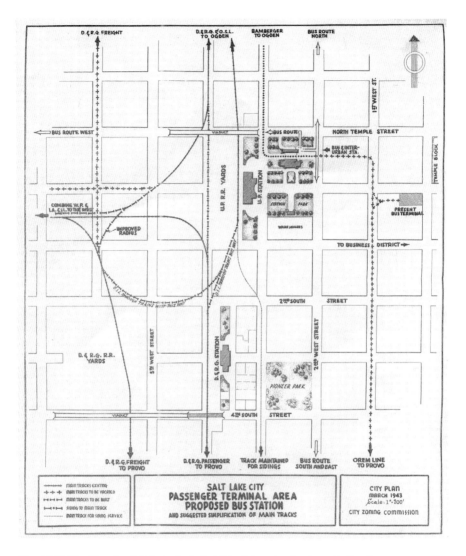

The 1943 City Plan for Salt Lake included this elaborate plan to revitalize the area near the Union Pacific Depot. *Salt Lake City Corporation.*

a $20 million transportation center at the site of the Union Pacific Depot that "would include facilities for air, rail and bus transportation, including a heliport and a high-speed monorail to shoot passengers out to the airport."[8] But these concepts stayed on the drawing table.

Had they been developed, however, they would have been mired in an inherent fallacy: that the depot itself would retain some kind of development value that could stimulate activity throughout the West End as a whole.

But the grand Union Pacific Depot was fast becoming an anachronism—a memorial of sorts to the days when trains were an integral part of American life. By 1925, the number of train passengers in the U.S. had peaked (with a brief spike in activity during World War II), and that decline in activity would substantially impact the West End. At the end of World War II, the block directly east of the depot, where two hotels and numerous small shops once thrived, was almost entirely vacant.

Over time, this malaise spread to the rest of the West End. Its increasing isolation happened gradually, but by 1962, it was so pronounced that the city's highly publicized "Second Century Plan" didn't even show the west end of South Temple. That area of town served conveniently as a placeholder for the map's label.

The construction in 1967 of a new civic auditorium—the "Salt Palace"—was accompanied by an almost unbounded (but, given the West End's history, misguided) optimism about its potential impacts on the west side of the city. The new arena was anticipated in much the same way that Station Park would have been had it been constructed. A 1964 *Deseret News* editorial projected hopefully that it "could help rehabilitate deteriorating parts of the downtown area."[9]

But the Salt Palace and related development couldn't counteract the West End's inertia. By 1975, it was once again a forgotten place. Nearly three-quarters of the block just west of Temple Square was dedicated to parking. The *entire* south side of the block was a surface parking lot. In the two blocks to the west, business activity had dwindled to the point at which fewer than 40 percent of the addresses were occupied. More than half of the properties were effectively vacant.

Vacancy was itself a natural outcome of isolation. The West End was literally a place apart, removed as it was from the areas of the city where growth was happening. And it was this geographic isolation that most profoundly influenced the West End's evolution, as evidenced by the story of one of the city's most iconic buildings: the Devereaux House.

When William Staines built "Salt Lake City's first mansion"[10] in 1857, the site he chose—on the fringes of the new settlement near 300 West—was downright idyllic with its pastures and trees and vistas across the valley. By the early 1870s, however, the mansion (now called "Devereaux House" by its current owner, William Jennings) had lost its pastoral solitude. The railroad had entered Salt Lake, routed less than a block west to the site of the Oregon Short Line Depot. Its proximity to the depot made the mansion the perfect venue for a reception center, and it became the social nexus for the

The Devereaux House as envisioned in its original pastoral setting. *Utah State Historical Society.*

city, as Jennings hosted a range of influential guests from Presidents Ulysses S. Grant and Rutherford B. Hayes to foreign dignitaries. Guest lists often numbered in the hundreds. For Salt Lake residents, the Devereaux House represented "quality and affluence at its best."[11]

But the end of the nineteenth century saw an apparent turn for the worse in the fortunes of the Jennings family. In 1903, the Devereaux House was purchased at a tax sale (a transaction analogous to a foreclosure) by investors Aaron Keyser and Thomas Weir. At the same time, the area around the Devereaux House had industrialized. The change in ownership and environment launched a new, unglamorous life for the Devereaux House. Over the next forty years, it diminished from Salt Lake's grand venue into a secluded rental property that would house an alcohol rehabilitation center, various residential tenants and—most significantly—the offices of an industrial equipment company.

The mansion's demotion only exemplified the broader changes occurring at the west end of South Temple. By 1925, nearly half of the properties in the block between 200 West and 300 West (now 300 West and 400 West) were empty lots. Buildings that remained were underutilized or vacant. The demolition of the Railroad Exchange Hotel in the 1920s and the Wellington Hotel (aka the Union Pacific Hotel) in the 1940s heralded the end of the railroad era in Salt Lake.

Ironically, it was likely the Devereaux House's extreme isolation (the *Deseret News* later characterized the mansion as "abandoned")[12] that helped to preserve it. Had this area evolved differently—had it, for example, become the intermodal hub envisioned in the 1943 City Plan—then real development pressures would likely have come into play. But the mansion, standing as it did at the end of what was literally and figuratively a dead-end street, was isolated—and insulated—from the kinds of changes that were occurring along South Temple east of West Temple, where new buildings were replacing old ones.

A 1978 retrospective described the desolate scene around the Devereaux House in the early 1900s: "[A]fter the Jennings family abandoned it, the mansion, standing as it did in an area trending toward industrial and commercial development, gradually slid from its place as a center of the city's social life to the ignominy of a decrepit dump, ripe for the wrecker's ball."[13] For most in the community, it had, by virtue of its isolation, become a place out of sight and out of mind.

But the mansion did have value for one person. Surrounded as it was by vacant property, it was the perfect site for a use that required ample space. Enter John Coan and his heavy equipment business. Incongruous as it may have seemed, the Devereaux House property offered Coan several distinct benefits. First, it was located near a rail spur, close to the Union Pacific Depot. So, transporting trucks and trailers and building materials (and, for a time, large quantities of coal) in and out would have been relatively easy. Second, the property occupied a large open lot, perfect for storing all manner of heavy equipment and supplies. Finally, the mansion itself provided a comfortable residence for John; his spouse, Emily; and their two children, Juanita and Glen.

For a time after Coan moved in with his business (and his family), the mansion and grounds retained much of their idyllic character in spite of the industrial use of the property. In later years, Glen would remember "the house and grounds being much as they must have been when the Jennings family lived there—wrought iron gates opening on a sweeping circular driveway, lawn and gardens in front with a fountain in the midst, Staines' fruit trees still growing in the side and back yards."[14] Eventually, however, gardens and fruit trees and fountains would give way to tractors and trailers and building supplies.

The offices of the J.J. Coan Wrecking Company in the once glamorous Devereaux House.
Utah State Historical Society.

While Coan and his family remodeled the interior fairly extensively, they left the exterior relatively untouched. To be sure, the Coans were not the most attentive caretakers, and the building did suffer some deterioration. Yet, in spite of its rather contrary evolution, it's important to note that the Devereaux House is the only building still standing on South Temple west of Temple Square—other than the Union Pacific Depot—that was built prior to 1972. In fact, it remains one of the oldest buildings on all of South Temple Street.

By the late 1960s, the Devereaux House was no longer out of mind. Various community groups began pointing to it as an important historic resource worthy of a collective preservation effort. In 1969, a committee of various community interests convened to develop a plan to restore the building, and in April 1979, the State of Utah purchased the mansion. However, the purchase and ultimate restoration of the Devereaux House did not change the fortunes of the West End. (In fact, following its restoration, the mansion itself would struggle to find an identity.) A restored Devereaux could not overcome the West End's geographic isolation. It was simply too far away from the city's center of activity.

The same could not be said about the Interurban Depot, constructed in 1923 on the southwest corner of South Temple and West Temple. It couldn't have been closer to Temple Square (unless, perhaps, it had been built right next to the Tabernacle), and downtown began just across the street. But its proximity to the city's centers of activity didn't stop its demise. Its isolation, like that of so many of the West End's buildings, wasn't geographic but functional. The Interurban Depot was, in fact, born into obsolescence.

That future could not have been envisioned by those attending the depot's opening in the fall of 1923, infused as it was with an expansive feeling of optimism about the potential of Utah's interurban rail lines and of the depot itself. With former governor Simon Bamberger as its principal developer, the new station promised that, as Bamberger himself put it, "as time goes on service will get better and better."[15] Bamberger had good reason to be optimistic. His Bamberger rail line had seen rapidly increasing ridership, and interurbans now extended both north and south along the Wasatch Front.

In 1933, the Interurban Depot was surrounded by its primary nemesis: automobiles. *Utah State Historical Society.*

Even as late as 1927, the *Ogden Standard* promoted the Salt Lake to Ogden line, observing that "the two largest cities, with a combined population of 170,000 in round numbers, have found the Bamberger Electric Railroad an invaluable asset to the community at large in the past score of years."[16] But that observation would be weighted with irony. When it was completed in 1923, the Interurban Depot was confronting its own demise. The automobile—not the train—would become the dominant mode of transportation for Utahns.

At its opening, however, the depot was perceived to be a permanent fixture along South Temple, standing as the physical symbol of the past and future success of the interurban lines in Utah. "With the completion of this depot," noted the *Salt Lake Telegram*, "the line will finally be finished, a recognized monument of efficiency in management, a record dividend earner, modern in every way as to equipment, shops, terminals, offices."[17] By all accounts, the new depot was a magnificent structure, even purported to be the finest in America. Designed by local architects Young and Hansen, it was large, with an expansive waiting room measuring 125 feet by 42 feet, and incorporated "every modern device."[18] Space was also provided for a restaurant, offices and retail shops.

But, perhaps a harbinger of the depot's impending obsolescence, the design had been substantially scaled back. An early drawing from 1914 (prior, even, to the construction of a temporary terminal building in 1916) shows a much more elaborate structure than the one that was eventually built, with a mansard roof, decorative columns and an ornamental balustrade along the roof line. What was constructed nearly ten years later was, by comparison, almost austere. Gone were the mansard roof and ornamental railing. While columns graced the South Temple entrance, they lacked the embellishment of those originally envisioned for the building. No clock presided over the door, as in the early design.

Nevertheless, the optimism surrounding the depot's opening was almost palpable. Two years before the building's completion, the *Salt Lake Telegram* noted that "an interesting feature in the construction of the new terminal is the provision that has been made for enlargement at any time the traffic may become heavy enough to warrant."[19] And a full ten years before the depot opened—before its location was even identified—local real estate agent J.L. Denham pronounced that "when the location of the new interurban depot is known it will not only stimulate the market in that vicinity, but also have a good effect on the general market."[20]

Denham's prediction reflected a widely held perception regarding the anticipated impacts of the new depot. So significant was its perceived value

PLANS COMPLETE FOR INTERURBAN TERMINAL STATION

JOINT ELECTRIC ROAD DEPOT WILL COST $200,000

WEST TEMPLE STREET ELEVATION OF PROPOSED INTERURBAN DEPOT.

·WEST·TEMPLE·STREET·ELEVATION·

This original drawing of the proposed Interurban Depot shows a much more elaborate building than the one that was eventually constructed. *Utah Digital Newspapers.*

that the LDS Church offered what was most likely the first development incentive in Salt Lake's history to locate the depot adjacent to Temple Square: the lot containing the Valley House Hotel on the southwest corner of South Temple and West Temple Streets. The business community was equally convinced. Anticipating a boom from the depot, downtown business owners matched the LDS Church's contribution of real estate with a $75,000 cash incentive to construct the depot on the Valley House site.

But the boom never materialized. Had the depot been constructed, say, twenty years earlier, when the interurban railways truly represented the future of transportation, the area around it may have developed in a significantly different way. However, less than thirty years after the opening of the depot, Utah's interurban lines were effectively extinct. In 1952, the Bamberger Rail Line carried its last passengers. The Interurban Depot's life as a train station had ended. Potential passengers had discovered a new, more convenient, more fashionable way to get around: the automobile. Its impact was immediate. In 1933, the Bamberger Rail Line went into receivership, and in 1944, the Salt Lake Terminal Company, the entity that owned the depot, followed suit.

But the end of interurban trains did not mean the end of the building. Even as the rail lines were being phased out, a new form of intercity transportation occupied the depot. Anticipating the demise of its rail lines, Bamberger Transportation had launched bus service throughout northern

Utah as a means of supplementing (and sustaining) its rail service. By the 1940s, Bamberger buses ran from the depot to various cities along the Wasatch Front.

Local bus lines, like Bamberger, were complemented by national bus lines. None other than the Union Pacific Railroad—perhaps recognizing the twilight of the passenger rail era—had created its own bus lines in 1927. In 1929, Union Pacific partnered with Chicago and North Western Railways to purchase Interstate Transit Lines, and in 1947, Interstate Transit Lines purchased the Salt Lake Terminal property. The Interurban Depot, ordained less than twenty-five years earlier to thrive indefinitely as a rail station, was now a bus station.

Although nominal owner of the depot, Interstate Transit Lines was by this time better known under its operating name: Greyhound Bus Lines. In assuming ownership and management of the depot, Greyhound went to great pains to establish a "new" identity for the depot building. Hiring the highly respected Salt Lake architecture firm of Ashton, Evans and Brazier, Greyhound undertook an extensive remodeling of the interior of the building.

When the Interurban Depot reopened as the Salt Lake Greyhound Bus Depot in 1949, it was hailed by the *Deseret News* as "Salt Lake's *newest* transportation facility, the *new* bus travel center." (author's emphasis) The paper went on to state that "the *new* bus terminal, one of the most *ultra-modern* in the West, represents a $400,000 improvement, including purchase of the old interurban terminal building from the Bamberger Railroad Company and a *complete remodeling* program."[21] Greyhound's own newspaper ad proclaimed that the building was a "beautiful *new* terminal."[22] (author's emphasis) To be sure, the interior was extensively remodeled and modernized. But the exterior remained essentially unchanged, save for new signs.

As with the opening of the Interurban Depot some twenty-five years earlier, Greyhound officials optimistically overestimated annual passenger arrivals and departures (at between 750,000 and 1 million). However, while Greyhound's operations remained profitable (primarily because of diversification into other industries), its passenger numbers declined in the face of intensifying competition from automobiles and from an emerging form of long-distance transportation: the airplane. In 1926, the Salt Lake City airport saw its first commercial passengers; less than twenty years later, it would report the seventh-largest passenger load in the country. Bus travel, however, would not follow the same trajectory. By the early 1960s, bus passengers for both major lines, Greyhound and Continental Trailways

When Greyhound Bus Lines moved into the Interurban Depot in 1949, it extensively remodeled the interior but changed very little on the exterior. *Utah State Historical Society.*

(which operated out of a different station), totaled only 700,000, less than half the projected ridership for Greyhound alone.

The depot had slipped into obscurity because of its increasing functional isolation. Its demise was representative of that of many of the properties in the West End. It simply wasn't useful. But the West End's segregation was also deeply affected by a more insidious form of isolation, one based on class and socioeconomic status.

The tale of this social isolation is told in the West End's numerous boardinghouses and bars. The former offered cheap, often temporary quarters for a mostly transient population associated primarily with the railroads. In some cases, they were stand-alone buildings, but more often they were tucked into the upper floors of buildings. Some were so inconsequential that they occupied "½" addresses.

This was a tough neighborhood. "Police Raid Two Hotels in Clean-Up Drive" was typical of the headlines coming out of the West End.[23] Petty crime was a way of life in the West End's hotels—larceny, burglary,

A 1914 view east toward Temple Square, looking through the tangle of low-rent hotels and bars. *Utah State Historical Society.*

gambling, etc. One newspaper account noted that the Ogden Hotel was raided an average of three times a month. Police raids were regular events, part of a "campaign to rid the city of undesirable characters."[24] Suicides were not uncommon. (Perhaps as a way to distance itself from the West End's rough-and-tumble nature, the Lucid Hotel advertised itself simply as a "clean, respectable place.")[25] Not surprisingly, bars were commonplace in the West End—Victory Lounge, Lone Pine Tavern and the Hurry Back Inn, just to name a few. Equally unsurprising, many of the West End's bars were also regular venues for petty crimes.

With rare exception, the residents and business owners of the West End were members of Salt Lake's disenfranchised community. They were not wealthy or powerful or famous. Because they were often transient occupants, whether as residents or as business owners, the West End didn't "belong" to them. They didn't have a sense of ownership over what might happen there—or even the leverage to influence it. So, in a very real sense, the area itself didn't belong to anybody who lived or worked there or even to the community as a whole.

The prevailing community attitudes about the area west of downtown, including the West End, were summed up in a 1962 report called the "Second Century Plan," which characterized it as "a mixed-indeterminate area": "This area west of the hard core, beginning with the line half a block west of

Main Street, is made up of low density retail-commercial warehousing, and industry westward to the band of industry along the railroad tracks. This is a generally deteriorating area from which the hard core is growing away."[26]

To its credit, the community refused to jettison the West End (and, more generally, the city's west side). Although the 1943 City Plan's Station Park concept and the transportation center envisioned by Ford Motor Company and United Airlines didn't pan out, the West End continued to be perceived as redeemable. By the mid-1960s, intensifying community interest in revitalizing downtown signaled significant changes for the West End. The focus of this particular redevelopment initiative was the design and construction of a "civic auditorium."

This was not a new idea. As early as the mid-1930s, the Salt Lake Chamber of Commerce had explored the potential for such a facility, creating a civic auditorium committee "to study the feasibility and advisability of constructing such a plant as part of the state's recovery program."[27] At various intervals over the next thirty years or so, the idea would be exhumed, examined and reburied—even though newspaper accounts of the various iterations regularly reported overwhelming support.

By the early 1960s, however, the civic auditorium concept had found what might be called a sense of urgency. A 1964 *Deseret News* editorial could hardly contain its enthusiasm, insisting that "it's hard to overestimate the importance of this project. It can shape this community's future in so many ways."[28] In the spring of 1966, after decades of deliberation, a civic auditorium was finally undertaken in Salt Lake City. Demolition was initiated on the buildings occupying Block 77—except, that is, for the Interurban Depot, which was retained as project headquarters during the demolition phase.

However, the reprieve for Bamberger's beloved station was short-lived. In July 1968, barely forty-five years after its construction, the Interurban Depot was demolished to make way for a nine-hundred-space surface parking lot that would serve the new civic auditorium, the Salt Palace. (Ironically, the Salt Palace would have a shorter life than the depot, standing only thirty-five years.) The depot's demise seemed to communicate the finality of the West End's isolation: "A chimney about 25 feet tall stood undamaged on the southwest corner of the building—a lonely reminder that activity once filled the depot."[29]

The end of one of its most significant buildings served as an appropriate metaphor for the increasing isolation of the West End—demolition to make way for, of all things, a parking lot. The site once projected as a busy hub for thousands of passengers now stood as an empty space, covered by asphalt, infrequently used. Yet, in a note of almost tragic irony, the Salt Palace was seen as the savior of the city's "mixed-indeterminate area." So much so that Salt Lake City commissioner Conrad B. Harrison waxed hyperbolic at the grand opening of the Salt Palace. "This is the greatest single development," Harrison exclaimed, "for the good of the Salt Lake area, and the core area particularly, in a hundred years."[30]

The Salt Palace was the key ingredient in a broader initiative to stimulate activity in downtown's west side. The other *big* component was a major hotel, the Howard Johnson Motor Lodge. Completed in 1972, the hotel, a restaurant and an accompanying parking garage occupied most of the north side of the block between West Temple and 200 West. The hotel was, by Salt Lake standards, a massive structure, towering thirteen stories over the West End. The parking garage alone was taller than nearly every other building that had ever stood in the West End. So momentous was the construction of this new hotel that none other than Utah governor Calvin Rampton and Salt Lake City mayor Jake Garn wielded sledgehammers in striking the ceremonial first blows of the demolition of the Marion Hotel that had stood at the site for over fifty years.

The goal of the new hotel was to provide rooms—lots of them—for what community leaders hoped would become a burgeoning convention business. A secondary goal was to stimulate activity in the West End—certainly in the area immediately surrounding the hotel. As with the Interurban Depot, however, Howard Johnson didn't "revitalize" the area. It was self-contained, and as with passengers exiting the Interurban Depot, its guests would have been inclined to turn toward Temple Square or saunter into downtown rather than turning west into the West End.

Even with all the "revitalization" ideas—envisioned and realized—the West End continued to languish. By 1975, only thirty-one addresses were occupied, less than a third of those that had been occupied only fifty years earlier. Much of the West End was simply empty—paved over for parking lots. The various ideas for its "revitalization"—a park, a transportation center, a civic auditorium, a conference hotel—were based on the misguided premise that a single project or a single building could, in and of itself, relieve the West End's isolation.

What they didn't take into account were the fundamental dynamics of the West End—or lack thereof. As late as 1980, even after the construction of Symphony Hall (Abravanel Hall) on the site formerly occupied by the Interurban Depot, the West End was described in much the same terms that had been applied in the city plan in 1943, as "a variegated strip of

A deserted landscape: South Temple between 200 West and 300 West, circa 1975. *University of Utah Marriott Library Special Collections.*

four blocks that is terminated by the main, old railroad station. The strip gradually declines from the attractive new Symphony Hall/Art Center and the Mormon Temple Square into a scene of bus stations, gas stations, parking lots, shops, bars, hotels, a used mining equipment yard and the abandoned but historic Devereaux House."[31]

2
THE CHURCH BLOCKS

Traditionalism, Modernism and Mormon Identity

It's no overstatement to say that Temple Square has always been the most recognizable address in Salt Lake City. In the early mapping of the city, it defined the axes from which north, south, east and west street numbers would proceed, and the growth of the city radiated from the intersection of Main Street and South Temple. For many years, virtually all of Salt Lake's major political, social and economic policies emanated from Temple Square.

Not surprisingly, then, the blocks immediately adjacent to Temple Square served as a model of Mormon identity. As downtown evolved, the two blocks along South Temple from West Temple to State Street, the "Church Blocks," increasingly reflected the seemingly disparate faces of the LDS Church. On the one hand, the still-young institution needed to project an identity of stability, gravity, permanence. On the other hand, the church's commercial enterprises that operated out of buildings across South Temple from Temple Square would feel increasingly compelled to communicate that they could change with the times.

Throughout the fifty years from 1925 to 1975, the northern nonsecular side of the Church Blocks stayed essentially the same. Temple Square itself experienced some change: a new visitors' center, information bureau building and annex. But because it was walled off from South Temple, it was—visually and functionally—a place apart from the street and the rest of the city. To the east lay "Administrative Square," with the grand Hotel Utah, the stately LDS Church Administration Building and the unassuming Lion House and Beehive House, all very much the same in 1975 as they were in 1925.

This northern half of the Church Blocks presented the LDS Church as an emerging religious institution—from its spiritual center at Temple Square to its administrative offices to the home of, arguably, its most influential leader. Together these buildings sought to demonstrate that the LDS Church had roots, solidity, a sense of permanence. The absence of change would have held tremendous symbolic value for the church's members, because it would have communicated a feeling of continuity within the institution. Born in turmoil and flight, the young church had settled in its adoptive home of Salt Lake barely three-quarters of a century earlier. In the 1920s, some members were likely still alive who had endured the harrowing trek across the plains in the late 1800s. So it would have been particularly important for the church to project, especially to its members, that it was steadfast.

The south side of the Church Blocks, however, would take on a very different character—even though it, too, was very much a part of the church's identity. Bordering downtown, its early significant structures—the Deseret News Building, the Vermont Building and especially the Templeton

The Templeton Building was one of the Church Blocks' grandest statements of commercial aspiration. *Utah State Historical Society*.

Building (all owned by the LDS Church)—expressed a contrasting set of aspirations. As the Church Blocks' north side remained a statement of clerical constancy, its south side transformed into a statement of commercial modernity.

However, the first buildings to appear in the Church Blocks after 1925 would have seemed only to reinforce the architectural status quo. Constructed independently of each other, the Medical Arts Building at 54 East South Temple and the Federal Reserve Bank just to the east at the corner of State Street and South Temple went up at virtually the same time. Individually and together, they announced that Salt Lake City was coming of age—that the once remote Mormon community had now achieved a worldly, more cosmopolitan status. (They would also be the only properties on the Church Blocks' south side not developed by the LDS Church.) Though they were touted by a local paper as "modern," they were very much statements of traditional architectural values.

The Medical Arts Building was the inspiration of Dr. Fred Stauffer, a Salt Lake eye, ear, nose and throat specialist, who significantly impacted the landscape of South Temple. In addition to being a physician, Stauffer was something of an entrepreneur. His business interests focused on real estate development, including construction of the eponymous Stauffer Apartments at 164 East South Temple in 1908. A *Deseret News* profile in 1903 described Stauffer as "a realty owner, who interests himself in every good work tending to the advancement of our city and its general prosperity."[32]

In 1925, Stauffer formed the aptly named Medical Arts Building Company, which purchased a lot from the LDS Church just west of the southwest corner of South Temple and State Street. Construction of the new Medical Arts Building began that fall with the demolition of the modest structure that had once housed the LDS Church historian's office. Designed by the Salt Lake architectural firm of Cannon & Fetzer, the new ten-story building was constructed of a relatively modern material: reinforced concrete. While local papers extolled its up-to-date features, in style it drew from the more popular conservative architectural influences of the time, particularly with its façade of polished granite, its ornate cornice gracing the roofline and an arcade of three grand arches projecting from the upper two stories on its north side.

The *Salt Lake Tribune* called the Medical Arts Building "a monument to the medical and dental profession of Salt Lake," proclaiming that it was "a building achievement which has placed Salt Lake on a par with 126 other cities of America, which contain office structures built for and occupied exclusively by members of the medical and allied professions."[33] The development of the Medical Arts Building not only set the standard for medical offices in Salt Lake but also established another milestone. Characterized as an "essential in modern medicine," a three-story parking garage accommodating one hundred cars was constructed behind the Medical Arts Building. A new use had arrived in downtown: the parking structure.

Even as it opened to great acclaim, however, the Medical Arts Building was deemed inadequate. Stauffer himself had asserted during construction that an additional one hundred offices could have been leased had there been space. So, in 1930, the Medical Arts Building Company set out to address the shortage. The solution was a massive addition that provided an additional forty-nine thousand square feet of office space, more than doubling the building's square footage. (The original building was thirty-two thousand square feet.) The annex extended south from the Medical Arts Building. Using the same materials, it was essentially indistinguishable from the original structure.

Meanwhile, next door to the east, a much smaller but nonetheless impressive structure was taking shape. The new Federal Reserve Bank at 70 East South Temple would occupy the former site of the Gardo House. However, this particular building would be significant not so much for its architectural as for its symbolic value.

The new bank would signify not the past but the future, manifesting Salt Lake's coming of age and its emerging role as a regional financial and business center. The decision by the Federal Reserve in 1918 to construct a bank in Salt Lake had validated the city's economic stature, for it would be the first in the Federal Reserve's twelfth district. "The Federal Reserve Bank of San Francisco," noted historians Thomas Alexander and James Allen, "recognized Salt Lake's regional predominance when, at the urging of Utah and southern Idaho bankers and the Salt Lake clearing house association, it established a branch bank in the capital city."[34]

Salt Lake architects Young and Hansen (who had also designed the Interurban Depot two blocks to the west) were selected to prepare plans for the building, which was projected to cost $250,000, excluding fixtures and vaults. "It is expected," wrote the *Salt Lake Telegram*, "that the building will be one of the finest and most complete branches of the federal reserve system in the country and will be an asset and a mark of beauty to Salt Lake."[35] Its design adapted traditional Neoclassical elements with more contemporary architectural ideas in a style that came to be known as "Stripped Classicism."

Completed in 1925, the Federal Reserve Bank (foreground) and Medical Arts Building began the transformation of the Church Blocks. *Utah State Historical Society*.

Like its neighbor the Medical Arts Building, the Federal Reserve Bank was characterized as "modern" at the time of its completion, prompting the *Salt Lake Telegram* to exclaim that "Modern Buildings Grace Landscape" and to praise the two structures as "monuments to the architectural beauty of Salt Lake."[36] Functionally they may have been modern, but architecturally they were very much steeped in more traditional styles with their historical references, such as the simple columns on the Federal Reserve Bank or the stone-clad façade of the Medical Arts Building. Their appearance suggested that the south side of the Church Blocks would ultimately carry through the architecture found along Temple Square and Administrative Square.

Two blocks to the west, on the southeast corner of South Temple and West Temple, another new building would only reinforce that perception. Although according to the *Salt Lake Tribune* it exemplified "the latest design and construction,"[37] the Temple Square Hotel would follow the examples of the Medical Arts Building and Federal Reserve Bank in echoing the

The Temple Square Hotel offered modern amenities in a rather traditional structure. *Utah State Historical Society*.

traditional architectural styles of the north side of the Church Blocks. Financed by the LDS Church and completed in August 1929, the Temple Square Hotel added nearly two hundred guest rooms immediately adjacent to Temple Square. The firm of Ashton & Evans designed the hotel with ornate flourishes. The first of its six stories was finished in marble, with arches over the South Temple entrance (eventually obscured by the hotel's marquee). The upper floors were clad in "tapestry" brick and trimmed in terra cotta. Projecting bays on its upper-floor framed windows were graced with decorative lintels. A three-story neon sign (if somewhat out of character then certainly ornate) hung on the hotel's northwest corner.

However, the opening of the Temple Square Hotel was less the beginning of an era than the end of one. For over forty years after the Temple Square Hotel welcomed its first guests, no new hotels would be constructed on South Temple—or even in the larger downtown. As late as 1955, the *Deseret News*, in an article reporting on the Temple Square Hotel's twenty-fifth anniversary, would tout it as "the Salt Lake City area's newest hotel."[38]

But the hiatus in construction in the Church Blocks was not limited to hotels. The brief flurry that had produced the Medical Arts Building, the Federal Reserve Bank and the Temple Square Hotel was just that—brief.

During the next twenty-five years, the Church Blocks would see the addition of only two new structures.

While certainly affected by the Great Depression, the pause in construction in the 1930s was a clear indicator of problems affecting the greater downtown. By the 1930s, Salt Lake's central business district was already glimpsing the end of its reign as the valley's center of commerce, and downtown (including the south side of the Church Blocks) would languish as new commercial centers sprouted around the valley. These new centers attracted the customers who had once patronized downtown businesses, because they had one key element that downtown lacked: parking.

Downtown wasn't ready for the impact of automobiles. It wasn't able to adapt to the immediate pressures that they exerted—pressures to accommodate them while they were moving *and* while they were stationary. The streets, wide as they were, couldn't be widened any more. And, since downtown was essentially built out, there weren't vast open spaces available in which to situate parking lots. Various articles and editorials agreed. The situation was catastrophic.

Given downtown's parking crisis, it was only natural that the only two structures constructed in the Church Blocks between 1930 and 1955 were parking garages. Ironically, the first, belonging to the Hotel Utah, was built not to respond to downtown's intensifying parking shortage but as a convenience for the hotel's guests. The garage opened in 1940, offering direct access to the hotel lobby, a turntable to facilitate entry and exit, 7,500-pound-capacity elevators that would lower and raise cars to and from the underground section "with speed and dispatch" and, of course, "garagemen" to park your car and, if necessary, service it while you were in the hotel.[39]

With only two hundred spaces—most occupied by the vehicles belonging to hotel guests—the garage did little to alleviate downtown's parking shortage. Its profile on South Temple was commensurately unsubstantial. Standing only one story, it was set well back from the street, tucked away just to the east of the massive hotel. It was the only visible (and barely visible at that) concession that the north side of the Church Blocks would make to changing times.

By the mid-1940s, downtown's lack of parking had escalated to something beyond a crisis. "With the parking situation in Salt Lake already 'acute,'" warned the *Deseret News* in 1945, "the expected increase in the number of motor vehicles with the coming of more gas, tires and automobiles may result in the situation becoming desperate."[40] It was clear that scattered small parking structures like those attached to the Medical Arts Building or the

The Hotel Utah parking garage (*lower right*) was the epitome of modern convenience, but it didn't solve downtown's parking crisis. *Utah State Historical Society.*

Hotel Utah or the Temple Square Hotel were simply inadequate to meet the demand. What was needed was a *big* solution.

The ZCMI parking "terrace," constructed in 1954, certainly was that. It was, in fact, huge. Five stories tall, it provided space for 550 cars. It was so large that the upper two floors of the ZCMI warehouse next door had to be removed to make room for its expansive parking decks. When it opened, it was the "largest ramp-type automobile storage structure in the Mountain West."[41]

Most important, however, was the new architectural standard set by the terrace. Visually, it was a striking departure from the other buildings of the Church Blocks. To South Temple, it presented a distinctly Modernist façade—all straight lines, rigidly geometric forms and no ornamentation. A set of rounded platforms projected from the center of the upper stories where ramps circled up the structure. "Sawtooth" roof lines with exposed structural steel rods along its side walls amplified the terrace's Modernist character.

So significant was the completion of the parking terrace that its opening was observed with a formal dedication presided over by none other than

With construction nearly complete, the ZCMI parking terrace displays some of the Modernist architectural ideas that would increasingly influence new buildings in the Church Blocks. *Utah State Historical Society.*

David O. McKay, president of the LDS Church. Mrs. Robert L. Judd Jr., representing "the fourth generation of one family to shop at ZCMI," cut the ceremonial ribbon. But the event carried broader, subtler implications. In his remarks, President McKay observed that the parking terrace was "indicative of the desire of the Church to keep ZCMI in tune with the times."[42]

The subtext in McKay's comment was all about the south side of the Church Blocks—the commercial face of the LDS Church. While the north, nonsecular side would remain resolutely unchanged, the south, secular side would modernize. For the LDS Church, the terrace represented an architectural leap and a clear statement that the Church Blocks' south side would assume a very different architectural personality than that of the north side. In many ways, McKay's statement wasn't so much of an observation as a directive and presaged an extensive modernization initiative that the LDS Church would undertake in the Church Blocks beginning in the late 1950s.

Touted as "ultra-modern" by the church-owned *Deseret News*, the ZCMI parking terrace was pronounced in a full-page grand opening ad purchased by ZCMI to be "years ahead of its time in design and function."[43] As well it should have been. Built only fourteen years after the Hotel Utah's "modern" parking garage and accommodating only slightly more than twice as many cars, the ZCMI parking terrace cost five times as much. Yet as expensive and innovative—as "ultra-modern"—as it may have been, it apparently wasn't that far ahead of its time. In 1971, less than twenty years after it opened, the ZCMI parking terrace would be demolished to make way for the ZCMI Center Mall (and an even larger parking structure).

But new parking garages could address only part of downtown's demise. That had as much to do with what was happening elsewhere as it did with what was happening in downtown itself. Suburban shopping centers were draining retail activity from downtown. Their attraction was twofold. Unlike downtown, they offered ample parking. But they were also modern, appealing to the changing consumer preferences associated with a new lifestyle emerging in the boom years following World War II.

Downtown, by contrast, was perceived as staid and old-fashioned. Its buildings were outdated—architecturally and functionally. As early as 1943, Salt Lake City government, in its first general plan, had recognized this inevitability: "Obsolescence of numerous existing structures and facilities in Salt Lake City will undoubtedly be hastened by post-war technological advances. Many of the City's office buildings, hotels, and apartments were built before 1910. Urban redevelopment on a broad scale, covering modernization or replacement of some of these older structures, would increase the economic efficiency of the City's physical plant."[44]

This observation certainly applied to the Church Blocks' south side, where venerable commercial structures owned by the LDS Church—including the Templeton Building, the Deseret News Building and the Vermont Building—manifested the very issues outlined by the city plan. Beautiful as they were, they did not readily accommodate changing office configurations and technologies. They were, distinctly, *not* modern. Yet despite the increasing pressures to modernize downtown and President McKay's decree, "modernization" was not a concept that the LDS Church would necessarily have embraced, even in its secular architecture. It was, after all, a conservative organization with conservative principles, and its ethic of traditionalist values was communicated through its architecture.

Although it had experimented on and off with contemporary architectural ideas of the twentieth century, the LDS Church had consistently reverted to more conservative architectural styles. Modernism was, if nothing else, a challenge to traditional aesthetic values that reflected deeper philosophical values. For many of the faithful, the LDS Church's Modernist experiments had struck at the very core. "To some observers," wrote historian Paul Anderson, "a style that grew partly out of the glorification of the machine presented problems for buildings that glorified other aspects of the human spirit."[45] Members of the LDS Church weren't necessarily alone in that assessment; Modernist architecture was not widely accepted throughout the United States.

Even with the pressure to show progress, it would have been quite natural for the LDS Church's commercial subsidiaries in the Church Blocks—ZCMI, Beneficial Life, Deseret Book and Zions Savings Bank & Trust Company—to stay comfortably housed in the old buildings that they had occupied for years. After all, they, too, were conservative institutions; their markets lay primarily in the church membership. The traditional image projected by those buildings—the Vermont or Templeton, for example—would have aligned with the conservative values of their customers. Yet the completion of the ZCMI parking terrace and President McKay's goal to "keep ZCMI in tune with the times" marked a clear turning point for the LDS Church's attitudes about how it presented its secular, commercial self.

This shift was manifested rather dramatically in the construction in 1955 of the new Beneficial Life offices at 57 West South Temple. Only a year earlier, the LDS Church had revealed its new architectural thinking in a remodel of Deseret Book at 44 East, which transformed the historic Deseret Sunday Union with a sleek, Modernist façade with large display windows framed in aluminum. However, those architectural ideas would be considerably amped up in the Beneficial Life Annex.

At the time, the company occupied neighboring buildings: the Vermont and the Sharon. The latter, built in 1890, had been purchased in 1907 by the LDS Church and remodeled to make it "thoroughly modern" and "up to date."[46] But 1907's "up-to-date" was 1955's *out*-of-date. So the venerable Sharon Building was demolished to make way for a very different structure. Although it was not particularly striking, the Sharon Building had an indisputable provenance, for it had been designed by perhaps the most significant architect in Utah history: Richard Kletting. Kletting had been the architect of, among others, several of the buildings along the University of Utah's Presidents Circle, the Wall mansion on South Temple and—most significant—the Utah State Capitol. Nevertheless, the Sharon Building's demise was met with a figurative shrug of the shoulders by the *Deseret News*, which remarked that "the old Sharon Bldg. went the way of all old buildings when a city progresses."[47]

The new building (referred to by Beneficial Life as an "annex" to its main offices in the Vermont Building next door) was, by any standard, strikingly Modernist. For the Church Blocks, it was a bold architectural gesture. Designed by Ashton Evans and Brazier, it stood in stark contrast to its neighbors—the Temple Square Hotel to the west (designed by the same firm) and the Vermont Building to the east.

Standing eight stories tall, it presented a façade with narrow aluminum columns framing a regular pattern of tall windows set off by porcelain enamel panels ("spandrels"). In appropriate Modernist fashion, its ornamentation was expressed not in applied embellishments (as with its neighbors the Vermont Building and Temple Square Hotel) but more subtly in the rectilinear form of the building and the contrast of materials. Imported granite, for example, trimmed the exterior in distinct variance with the modern materials on the rest of the structure. Architecturally, it was very much of its time, the consummate expression of corporate efficiency.

The *Deseret News* raved about the Beneficial Life Annex. The building, proclaimed the paper, was "[a]n Industrial Monument."[48] Nearly thirty years later, a retrospective about the company continued to extol the building's uniqueness. "The gleaming exterior of the new building," remarked the history, "symbolized 52 years of Beneficial progress."[49]

Unfortunately, as with the ZCMI parking terrace, the *Deseret News* also characterized the Beneficial Life Annex as "ultra-modern," a label that did not bode well. Less than twenty years after its completion, it no longer suited the needs of the company for which it had been built and after which it was named. In 1975, Beneficial Life moved into a new building—the Beneficial Life Tower at the east end of the brand-new ZCMI mall—that, while not "ultra modern," was "as modern and efficiently effective as any company offices in the land."[50]

Spurred, perhaps, by the success of its early forays into Modernist design along the Church Blocks, the LDS Church dramatically expanded its modernization efforts. In October 1958, L. Pierce Brady, general manager of Zions Securities (the church's real estate development subsidiary), presented a plan to create a "civic center and heart"[51] for Salt Lake City by transforming the area around Temple Square into a complex of church and government buildings. The church's plan included construction of several large buildings for its own purposes: an auditorium north of Temple Square with a capacity of twenty-five to thirty thousand; a new archives building on the northeast corner of North Temple and Main Streets; and a ten-story office building on the southeast corner of South Temple and Main Streets. In his presentation, Brady noted that the church's long-range plan for the area included two projects already completed: the ZCMI parking terrace and the Beneficial Life Annex.

Although the plan stumbled on issues related to property exchanges, the church forged ahead with the overall concept, which had—even with various setbacks—become even more ambitious. The revised version included not only the new archives building but also a thirty-eight-story building for the church's administrative offices, a seventeen-story annex to the Hotel Utah, a new and improved Deseret Gymnasium, a larger Temple Annex building and the persistent ten-story office building. In 1962, however, just as construction on the new administrative office building was about to launch the revised plan, church leadership abruptly cancelled plans for construction of the new archives building.

With all the uncertainty in which it was now immersed, the entire strategy seemed on the verge of collapse. Yet the concept of the modest ten-story office building concept not only maintained—it also grew in stature. The structure that eventually rose on the southeast corner of Main and South Temple Streets would be substantially taller and more elaborate than the one originally conceived.

However, creating space for it required the demolition of the showiest building in the Church Blocks: the Templeton. Constructed in 1889, it, too, had an impressive architectural pedigree. Its designer, Joseph Don Carlos Young, had been the architect for the LDS Church, responsible for the final design of the Salt Lake Temple as well as for the LDS Church Administration building at 47 East South Temple. Yet as with the demolition of the Sharon Building only a few years earlier, the prevailing sentiment for the Templeton's demise amounted only to what might be called a wistful pragmatism, as reflected in a 1960 *Deseret News* headline: "S.L. Landmark Makes Way for Progress."[52] Grand as it was, the Templeton would pale in size and presence to the structure that would replace it. That the new building would be ostentatious was perfectly understandable. Its namesake, the Kennecott Corporation, was, at the time of its construction, riding the crest of a wave of prosperity.

Started in Alaska in the early 1900s, Kennecott Mines Company grew rapidly. In 1915, it purchased a 25 percent interest in the Utah Copper Company, which operated a mine in Bingham Canyon on the west side of the Salt Lake Valley. By 1936, Kennecott owned all of Utah Copper's assets outright. World War II was a lucrative period for the company, which set production records at the Bingham Canyon mine, and demand for its minerals kept peaking through the mid-1950s.

Mining was woven into the fabric of Utah culture, and the company itself had by this time become an integral element of Utah's economy. When its new offices rose on the corner of South Temple and Main Streets, Kennecott managed the state's largest payroll and employed more workers than any other private enterprise. The new building at the corner of South Temple and Main Streets represented a grand tribute to the significance of the mining industry—and to Kennecott. Columnist Jack Goodman would later observe that "as for the Kennecott Building, its copper-covered panels spoke, rather ostentatiously, for the metal-mining industry that forged mid-century Utah, a state whose old agricultural way of life was efficiently ousted, seemingly forever."[53]

As productive as digging into a mountainside might have been for Kennecott, digging into a comparatively small site for its new building was another matter entirely. Following the demolition of the Templeton Building in 1959, workers immediately began excavation for the new building. However, construction was just as immediately delayed by various setbacks. The site flooded. Workers went on strike. Most significant of all, however—the building was completely redesigned.

The original plans, drawn up by the ubiquitous Ashton, Evans & Brazier, envisioned a building rising seventeen stories. The second and third floors formed a base that projected from the rest of the building and was faced with contrasting architectural stone, giving the appearance that the upper floors were floating above. Although the building would be named after Kennecott, the plan was for the ZCMI department store to occupy the first four floors—more space, actually, than allocated to Kennecott.

What happened next, however, was, to say the least, unexpected, especially given the fact that the Kennecott Building's primary tenant (ZCMI) and its developer (Zions Securities) were, in effect, subsidiaries of the same entity (the LDS Church). Rather abruptly, ZCMI changed its plans, announcing in April 1961 that it would expand its existing Main Street store rather than moving into the space in the Kennecott Building. According to Harold Bennett, ZCMI president, "The needs of the Kennecott Building and ZCMI were not architecturally 'compatible.'"[54] Bennett did not elaborate.

The impact of ZCMI's decision on the design of the Kennecott Building was sudden and dramatic, significantly altering the building's proposed use, particularly in the lower floors, which were to have been occupied by the store. Ashton, Evans & Brazier had, quite literally, to go back to the drawing board. The *new* new building would require, according to the *Salt Lake Tribune*, "an entirely new architectural approach."[55]

This "new architectural approach" caused the building's profile to change completely. Its South Temple frontage was reduced. To compensate, it grew taller—to eighteen stories. As a result, it became more distinctly vertical in appearance. Gone was the base of architectural stone. The second and third stories no longer projected from the rest of the structure. What remained was a tall, narrow structure.

Construction on the *new* new building finally commenced early in 1963, three years after the demolition of the Templeton Building and a year after construction of the original design was to have been finished. With all its setbacks, however, the Kennecott Building would live up to the company's own ordination of it as a "gleaming copper landmark."[56] Sitting on six hundred steel piers driven seventy feet below basement level, the building soared above its downtown neighbors. (For a few short years, it would stand as the tallest building in the city.) It was, quite appropriately, the world's largest copper-sheathed building, faced with 600,000 pounds of the metal. The copper itself was finished with "a transparent protective porcelain coating, the first such use in building construction."[57] White cast-stone columns extended the entire height of the building. In between, six-foot windows were framed by copper panels that were framed, in turn, by bronze mullions.

The Kennecott Building opened in 1965 to great acclaim—at least from Kennecott itself, which proclaimed that "no other building in the West has achieved such architectural distinction"[58] and called the structure "a testimonial to the beauty and durability of the everlasting metal."[59] Unfortunately for the Kennecott Building, at the same time that Kennecott was characterizing its new offices as "everlasting," the *Deseret News* was labeling them "ultra-modern."[60] The Kennecott Building would share with its "ultra-modern" siblings, the Beneficial Life Annex and the ZCMI parking terrace, the unenviable status of an abbreviated life, standing for barely forty years before undergoing an extensive remodeling. The "everlasting metal" wouldn't be. In 2007, it would be replaced with a contemporary skin.

By the time that Kennecott's workers were settling into their new offices in 1965, the LDS Church's modernization initiative was in full swing. Although its plan for a "civic heart" for Salt Lake City failed to materialize (at least, on

The Kennecott Building was a dramatic architectural homage to its namesake. *Utah State Historical Society.*

the scale originally envisioned), it had, within the last ten years, modernized nearly half of the Church Blocks. According to historian John McCormick, during the 1960s, "more money was poured into concrete, steel, and mortar than during any previous period, and the LDS church was deeply involved in changing the city's face."[61] The completion (finally) of the Kennecott

Richard Kletting's graceful design for the Deseret News Building produced "the handsomest structure in the intermountain region." *Utah State Historical Society*.

Building would only intensify the momentum that would carry across Main Street to affect one of the Church Blocks' most venerable buildings.

Named for the *Deseret News* at its completion in 1902, the structure on the southwest corner of Main Street and South Temple shared the Sharon Building's architectural pedigree. In this earlier building, Richard Kletting had designed a graceful six-story structure with a refined rounded corner facing the intersection. Its most distinctive feature was a series of grand four-story arcades framed by decorative columns that rounded off in arches on the fifth floor. At the building's completion, the *Deseret News* (unencumbered, it appears, by a conflict of interest) called it "the handsomest structure in the intermountain region."[62]

But handsomest in 1902 had, sixty years later, faded to unattractive. Rather, the building had, according to the *Salt Lake Tribune*, "long presented a stone face to the public."[63] So it was in 1965 that it went through a dramatic makeover and was covered with what columnist Jack Goodman would later describe as "vertical bands of black and white metal."[64] The *Salt Lake Tribune*

By the mid-1960s, even the "handsomest structure" in the Church Blocks had undergone a dramatic modernization. *Utah State Historical Society.*

hailed the fact that, as it saw it, the Deseret News Building would now be cloaked "in gleaming white."[65]

As intensive as the LDS Church's modernization program might have been through the 1950s and 1960s, all that concrete and steel would be trivial compared to the amount used in a single project undertaken by the LDS Church in the mid-1970s. Given its scale, it's not surprising that this new structure took years to materialize.

ZCMI's withdrawal from the Kennecott Building had not been nearly as auspicious for ZCMI as it had for Kennecott. ZCMI's plans for a new building on Main Street had stalled, undergoing revision after revision. When Harold Bennett had announced the withdrawal in 1961, he had presented an alternate plan for development of a new ZCMI complex on Main Street that would include an "L-shaped mall" to the south of the Kennecott Building and a new headquarters for the company to the south of the mall. The mall would be substantial—400,000 square feet—adding about 30 percent more space to the store itself and 350 spaces to the ZCMI parking terrace. By 1963, however, the project appeared to be moving backward. ZCMI's annual report of that year made only a passing reference to it, noting that "architecture and land utilization studies are continuing leading to the final plans for the new downtown store."[66] For the next six years, the concept went dark. Principals of ZCMI fell silent.

In 1969, Harold Bennett broke the silence, announcing to shareholders that, instead of a larger new store, the company would build a huge multimillion-dollar shopping mall. The complex would be five times as large

Downtown Salt Lake being "gouged out" to make way for the ZCMI Center Mall. *Utah State Historical Society.*

as the 400,000-square-foot building originally contemplated for the site. As if a 2-million-square-foot mall weren't enough, the massive development would include a twenty-story office building and a two-thousand-car parking structure to replace the ZCMI parking terrace constructed only fifteen years earlier.

The ZCMI Center Mall, as it would be named, embodied the conventional wisdom of the time: that revitalizing downtown required an immediate, comprehensive solution. Tear everything out and replace it with something new. The *Salt Lake Tribune* provided a dramatic description of the process: "Almost the entire 10-acre block between State and Main and South Temple and First South is being gouged out."[67]

"Gouged" was an understatement. The razing of the ZCMI parking terrace alone entailed what was characterized as "the largest single wrecking operation using explosives in Utah history."[68] (Even in its demise, the parking terrace was still establishing milestones.) The operation once again changed the face of the south side of South Temple between Main and State Streets, clearing the entire middle of the block for what would eventually be the north entrance to the mall.

Construction of the mall began in 1971 and took four years. Forty miles of steel pilings supported the windowless "megastructure," which was faced with precast architectural concrete. Seventy-five thousand cubic yards of concrete were poured. Inside, ZCMI was complemented by sixty other stores. Shoppers strolled about in a climate-controlled environment landscaped with fountains, shrubs and benches. One of the mall's special highlights was the new parking structure with an entrance on South Temple. It held nearly four times as many cars as the earlier parking terrace and added its own modernistic features, including signals indicating where parking spaces were available. By the time the project was completed, the price tag had escalated from the original $30 million to $50 million (about $290 million in 2015 dollars). No wonder. ZCMI Center was, at its opening in 1975, the largest indoor shopping mall in the country.

Naturally, superlatives abounded. Deemed by the *Salt Lake Tribune* as "probably the most exciting commercial environment in any American city," the mall was seen as downtown's salvation. The *Tribune* euphorically predicted that "the long-term impact of the mall will be significant."[69]

However, as big and grand and elaborate as the ZCMI Center might have been, it was not big or grand or elaborate enough to withstand changing patterns in retailing and shopping. Within twenty years, the excitement would fade. By the turn of the twenty-first century, the "most exciting commercial environment" had become, most of the time, the emptiest commercial environment. Barely thirty years old, the ZCMI Center Mall would be demolished in 2006 to make way for the newest generation of shopping malls: the City Creek Center.

For the time being, however, the ZCMI Center Mall announced its presence on South Temple with a metal-and-glass façade that housed "a new, glistening-bright atrium and food park."[70] But the modern façade was framed with cast-stone columns, a nod (or concession) perhaps to the traditional buildings across the street.

Or perhaps it was an homage to the buildings that had been replaced on the south side itself. For the opening of the ZCMI Center capped an extraordinary period on the south side of the Church Blocks. By 1975, only one major building on the south side—the Vermont—would be left standing as it was in 1925. (However, it, along with a set of modest storefronts just to the east, would soon be demolished to make way for Crossroads Mall.) By 1975, carved stone and elaborate ornamentation had been replaced with sleek aluminum and smooth surfaces. The architectural influence was distinctly Modernist.

By contrast, that influence would be noticeably absent on the Church Blocks' north side. To be sure, the church did construct new buildings on Temple Square. A temple annex and visitor center were constructed in the mid-1960s. The latter suggested a Modernist aesthetic with plain, white, unadorned walls and a semicircle of metal-framed windows. But the impact of these two structures on South Temple itself would be minimal, because they sat behind the massive wall surrounding Temple Square.

In a brief span of fifty years, the Church Blocks had come to adopt two very different personalities. The north side—Temple Square and Administrative Square—looked almost exactly the same as it did in 1925. In its unchanging nature, it was resolute, communicating an identity of the LDS Church as a steadfast institution, always there for the faithful. As the north side's buildings aged, they assumed a stately demeanor, reinforcing architecturally the enduring traditional values of the church.

The south side, by contrast, displayed the church's secular identity. By 1975, that identity had assumed the character of gleaming, Modernist façades. Those façades communicated very different ideals from their counterparts across South Temple, ideals of corporate efficiency and innovation. "Our buildings are state-of-the-art, and so are our companies," they seemed to say. In stark contrast to the north side, the south side stood not as a monument to permanence but as a testament to progress.

3

THE LOWER EAST

A Jumble of Coexisting Uses

In 1907, John Sharp constructed a "modern and up-to-date apartment house" on the northwest corner of South Temple and E Street.[71] While he may not have thought of himself as such, Sharp was something of a pioneer. Although no apartment buildings had been constructed this far east on South Temple, Sharp Flats' pioneering quality lay not so much in its geography as in its varied use. For the ground floor would be occupied not by residents but by businesses.

The term "mixed-use" had yet to enter the urban planning vocabulary, but John Sharp's modest development project introduced commercial uses to what, at the time, appeared to be maturing into a residential area. But it would develop into something quite different. Sharp Flats stood at the east end of a four-block stretch from State Street to 500 East—the "Lower East"—that would, between 1925 and 1975, assume a diverse character, incorporating, somewhat awkwardly, an incongruous assortment of uses, including social clubs, medical buildings, apartment buildings, office buildings, retail stores, churches, homes and vacant lots.

As much as any other area along South Temple, the Lower East would come to manifest the challenges of change along South Temple. Its evolution would prompt a collective wringing of hands, as residents and city officials alike decried the increasing intrusion of commercial activity between State Street and 500 East and the loss of residential character along those four blocks. But the premise that drove that anxiety—that the Lower East was an inherently residential neighborhood (i.e., made up primarily of single-

Sharp Flats extended the presence of commercial development to 500 East in the early 1900s. *Utah State Historical Society*.

family homes)—was misguided. To be sure, there were clusters of houses on either side of South Temple between State Street and 500 East, so the casual observer might easily have perceived them to be homes. By 1925, however, many had already been converted to other nonresidential uses. The Frank Jennings home at 111 East had become a tavern. The Newhouse mansion a few doors to the east served as the Knights of Columbus hall. Larkin Mortuary operated out of the Frank Hagenbarth residence at 260 East. The Bernard Schettler home at 347 East housed various auxiliary functions of the Cathedral of the Madeleine.

Current-day planners would call these transformations "adaptive reuse," the conversion of an existing building to a completely different use. Through the process of adaptive reuse during the early twentieth century, the Lower East had been diversified, diminishing whatever single-family residential character it may have ever had. As early as 1910, nearly half of the properties in the Lower East were used for purposes other than as single-family homes.

This early diversification was fostered by scale—or, more precisely, lack thereof. A truly residential neighborhood of single-family homes is

The Buckingham Apartments and its sibling, the Covey Apartments (*far left*), dwarfed neighboring buildings, reflecting the Lower East's disparity of scale. *Utah State Historical Society.*

defined primarily by a consistency in scale, a sameness in the size of the lots and in the size of the houses. But lots and structures in the Lower East varied significantly in size. The Newhouse mansion at 165 East sat on a lot that was 50 percent larger than the lot to the west and three times the size of the lot to the east. Between 300 East and 400 East, the Barbara Worth Apartments and Crestholme Apartments occupied two lots that were larger than the four lots immediately to the east put together. And those four lots collectively would have fit nicely into the single lot occupied by the Wall mansion at 411 East.

Structures were equally unequal in scale. At 239 East, the immense Covey Apartments rose seven stories. Next door, the Buckingham Apartments, four stories tall, sprawled on a footprint twice that of the Covey Apartments. Yet just across the street side sat a row of five diminutive homes. Between 300 East and 400 East, the Cathedral of the Madeleine and First Presbyterian Church on the north side of South Temple towered over the houses on the south side.

The disparity of scale and diversity of use defined the Lower East from its earliest days. Because sizes and functions of buildings were so varied, there was little if any sense of coherence. This disunity instilled the Lower East with instability, sowing the seeds of change. For this was a place without an established identity—functionally or visually.

There was yet another factor that affected the nature of change in the Lower East: its adjacency to downtown. By 1925, the Lower East had evolved into a transitional zone between the commercial and business center of downtown and the stately boulevard of mansions and estates to the east. In the early 1900s and into the 1920s, Salt Lake City was growing rapidly. Its urban core—its downtown—was growing accordingly. That growth naturally stimulated ancillary activity in adjacent areas—smaller-scale commercial, "urban residential" (i.e., apartments) and so forth. The Lower East was prime territory for this type of growth.

Over the next fifty years, the Lower East would change into what might best be described as a "varied-use" district—a little of this, a little of that. One block between State and A Streets would be known for a time as the "club district."[72] No wonder. Here sat the prestigious Alta and University Clubs, as well as the Elks Building and the Knights of Columbus hall. Two blocks east lay what could just as easily have been called the "church district," with the majestic Cathedral of the Madeleine, the massive First Presbyterian Church and ancillary church buildings dominating the landscape. In between and all around were scattered buildings of various sizes, shapes and uses—and empty spaces of no use at all.

The impact of vacant lots on the Lower East's identity crisis can't be overstated. Between 1925 and 1950 alone, fully one-third of all properties in the Lower East would, at one time or another, sit idly as empty spaces. Demolitions were common. So common, in fact, that they didn't merit the attention of local newspapers.

By 1940, nearly half of the square footage on the north side of South Temple between State and A Streets comprised vacant lots. In the east half of the block, four homes had been demolished, leaving the Knights of Columbus hall to survive stubbornly (and somewhat forlornly) among veritable fields of blank space (expediently converted to parking lots). Yet even that stately structure was demolished in 1960 to make way for… nothing. Vacant lots were black holes, draining the energy out of whatever opportunity the Lower East might have had to establish a clear identity.

Needless to say, the community generally was confused by these four blocks. Were they residential? Were they commercial? Would they (should they) be dedicated to another set of uses? Clubs? Churches? Apartments? The debate as to just what the blocks between State Street and 500 East were or should be would become so intense that in 1934 it would prompt one exasperated member of the Board of Adjustment to figuratively throw up his hands and pronounce that the community needed to fish or cut bait and choose definitively whether these four blocks would be "zoned once and for all time either commercial or residential."[73]

Zoning would certainly play a role in how the Lower East evolved. More than any other stretch along South Temple, it was the subject of intense scrutiny and heated argument. For many, commercialization was apocalyptic. For others, stasis meant stagnation. In 1935, following a vigorous debate, the Salt Lake City Commission approved a change in zoning along South Temple between State Street and 500 East that expanded the list of allowable activities to include a varied list of commercial uses.

At its enactment, however, this change was less of a proactive measure than a ratification of existing commercial activity. As noted above, diversification had been creeping into the Lower East almost since the street was platted. Even as early as 1925, less than 50 percent of the properties were occupied by homes, making it hard for the most adamant opponents of commercialization to argue that this was a single-family neighborhood. Small clusters of houses—groupings of four or five together—could be found, but the landscape of the west end of the Lower East would, by the late 1920s, come to be dominated by a different kind of residence: apartments. In 1925, nearly 20 percent of all properties were apartment buildings—that is, buildings constructed specifically to house apartments—and by the mid-1930s, they represented the most common use in the entire Lower East. Apartments were a natural development here, an ancillary impact of the increasing density of activity in downtown. As an urban form of residential space, they were better suited to the periphery of a busy downtown than were houses. And their proliferation reflected the changes in apartment living.

For Salt Lake's early apartment dwellers, luxury had been the byword. The Bransford Apartments, for example, on the northeast corner of South Temple and State Street were as extravagant when they were built in 1905 as any of the grand mansions to the east. By the mid-1920s, however, extravagance was giving way to expedience. Convenience, not luxury, became the byword of apartment living. The market for apartments had expanded significantly and now included a broader, less wealthy demographic. To meet the increased demand and accommodate lower incomes, modest buildings appeared, offering smaller, more affordable apartments.

The extravagant Bransford Apartments offered apartment living at its most luxurious. *Utah State Historical Society*.

The Manor Apartments, constructed in 1925 at 283 East, represented this new generation of apartment buildings. It replaced a grand Victorian mansion built in 1883 by Judge Robert Harkness with a structure that, aside from its stately entry, was rather plain—a concession to the primacy of economy over extravagance. Its apartments each contained only three or four rooms.

Just as the Manor was opening, construction was underway at 140 East on the Federal Hotel Apartments (so called because of its proximity to the Federal Reserve Bank Building). The Federal Hotel held fifty-eight apartments—ten more than the massive Buckingham, eighteen more than the massive Bransford and a whopping thirty-one more than the not-so-massive Manor. But the number was telling. Three-quarters of these "apartments" were simply single rooms with a bath. Only fourteen had two or more rooms. Not surprisingly, the Federal Hotel Apartments' grand opening ad in 1926 did not speak to the luxury of the accommodations. Rather, it emphasized their modern conveniences, including Electric Ranges and Electric Refrigerators (prominently capitalized).

By the late 1920s, when the Federal Hotel Apartments (later renamed the Carlton Hotel) were constructed, apartment design focused on convenience rather than luxury. *Utah State Historical Society.*

Yet a third small, plain apartment building would, at the same time, substantially accelerate the momentum of apartment construction in the Lower East. Built by husband-and-wife developers Frank and Zella Roberts, the Roberta Apartments (named after their youngest child) reinforced the theme articulated by the Manor and Federal Hotel Apartments. It was small (thirty four-room apartments) and modest, the only ornamentation being the stonework framing the front entrance.

If the Federal Hotel, Manor and Roberta Apartments demonstrated a changing set of values toward apartment living—one that favored economy and convenience over luxury and prestige—then the new apartment building that rose at 326 East in 1931 might be said to have re-instilled at least the romance of apartment living. Named after the title character in a popular 1911 melodrama, the Barbara Worth Apartments were constructed by the Doxey-Layton Company, an established Salt Lake real estate development firm that would later construct the Doxey-Layton Medical Center just a couple of blocks to the east. The building's Tudor Revival style evoked the romance of Elizabethan England with its half-timbering and an elaborate entry graced by a stone arch.

Even though it was small in scale, the Barbara Worth Apartments reintroduced romantic architectural ideas to apartment design in the Lower East. *Utah State Historical Society.*

By this time, it might have appeared to the casual observer that the Lower East was transforming into an apartment borough. That perception would only have been reinforced in 1931 with the construction of the Crestholme Apartments at 454 East (just east of the Roberta). The Crestholme followed what was by this time the accepted model. It was relatively small and relatively simple, standing three stories tall and containing forty-one apartments. Yet surprisingly, with all this momentum in apartment development (five new buildings in the Lower East in only five years), the Crestholme turned out to be the last new apartment building constructed in the Lower East for over fifty years.

Nevertheless, the impact of this flurry of apartment construction was significant, for it fueled the ensuing commercialization of the Lower East. Granted, the process of commercialization would not—could not—have happened without the enabling zoning ordinance passed in 1935. But "apartmentization" substantially altered the dynamics of the Lower East, because it significantly increased the density of activity in the blocks between State Street and 500 East—more people, more cars, more hustle and bustle.

Apartments had, since the passage of the first zoning ordinance, been an allowed use in the Lower East. Even as the new ordinance was passed in 1935, this was already an area trending toward a higher density of use and trending away from any future (however remote) as a single-family residential neighborhood.

Ironically, although these new apartment buildings would significantly alter the Lower East's patterns of activity, their visual impact was substantially less dramatic. The tallest stood only four stories, hardly taller than the Daly mansion at the corner of South Temple and B Street or the Wood mansion at 273 East. For the most part, they were constructed on narrow lots, so their façades had essentially the same street frontage as that of larger residences. And they incorporated materials and styles found in the Lower East's homes. Paradoxically, at the same time that these new apartment buildings were changing the dynamics of the Lower East, they were, in many ways, reinforcing the perception that it was a single-family neighborhood.

Even without new construction, a different form of apartment building would amplify the presence of apartments in the Lower East. Between 1925 and the end of World War II, over 20 percent of the homes in the Lower East would be converted into apartment houses, including notable residences such as the Daly mansion and the Ferry mansion at 453 East. (The original University Club Building at 136 East also incorporated apartments in the 1950s toward the end of its existence.) As with the construction of new apartment buildings, however, the conversions happened within a relatively narrow band of time. At the end of World War II, even as the demand for housing in Salt Lake was skyrocketing, the alteration of homes to apartments abruptly ceased.

Nevertheless, the conversion of homes, like the construction of new apartment buildings, substantially affected the dynamics of the Lower East. First, it removed the houses from use as single-family residences. Second, it further intensified the density of activity. By the end of World War II, apartment structures of all kinds (apartment buildings, apartment houses and boardinghouses) constituted the primary use in the Lower East.

There were now exponentially more residents in the four-block area than there had been only a decade or two before. More than anything else, these new residents would transform what might have felt like a relatively quiet, almost suburban setting into a busy, urban environment. Some viewed this transformation as a welcome change. As early as 1926, real estate agent Robert Nowell had extolled the virtues of "the changing character of South Temple street." "In the last few years," Nowell remarked, "this street has become a magnet for apartments and club buildings." "With proper restrictions," Nowell concluded, "this street should become a high-class club and apartment building center."[74]

But for Nowell and others who shared his vision, the devil would lie in that qualifier: "with proper restrictions." As the density increased in the Lower East, so, too, did the pressure to open the area to a broad range of development. Increasingly confronted by variance requests to expand permitted uses, in 1934 the City Commission took up the issue of rezoning the four blocks to allow commercial buildings to locate alongside residential ones.

The commission was presented with what the *Salt Lake Telegram* characterized as a "knotty problem." "Many individuals interested in city planning have described East South Temple street as the future location of fine apartments and fine apartment hotels. With that and other noncommercial purposes in view they have advised against commercial invasion of the thoroughfare predicted to one day become a boulevard and showplace of the city." There was, however, the contrasting perspective quoted above, held by those who "declare the property is no longer saleable with the present bans against business use of the street. They point to its desirability for smart shops and to the valuable property now lying idle and constituting eyesores along one of the principal traffic arteries serving the eastern residential section."[75]

By 1935, the City Commission was clearly feeling the pressure. Although the Lower East was zoned "B-2," with only residential uses (house, apartments and "hotels") permitted, commissioners had fielded a veritable barrage of petitions for variances (exceptions to the ordinance). While the City Commission ultimately denied a healthy share of these petitions, the reality was that the Lower East was commercializing incrementally through the granting of variances.

To its opponents, the prospect of this zoning revision was nothing short of apocalyptic. The natural outcome would be a street of "filling stations, hamburger and hot dog stands and other undesirable enterprises."[76] Nevertheless, the City Commission passed the amendment in 1935, permitting a broad set of uses, including retail businesses, drugstores, bank and office buildings, barber and beauty shops, theaters, restaurants and tearooms and gas stations.

Surprisingly (more so, perhaps, to its opponents than to anyone else), the new zoning change did not instigate a commercial invasion. In fact, in the ten years following the rezoning, only ten properties—slightly more than 10 percent of all the properties in the Lower East—converted to commercial use. Apocalyptic prophecies notwithstanding, the process of commercialization in the Lower East did not immediately change its nature. It wasn't until the mid-1950s that commercial business would constitute the primary use in the Lower East. Even then, it ranked only slightly higher than apartments. The wasteland of "filling stations, hamburger and hot dog stands and other undesirable enterprises" simply didn't materialize.

That's not to say that change didn't occur as a result of the 1935 zoning amendment. Most assuredly it did. But, as much as anything else, the amendment served to ratify a process of commercialization through variances that would have continued because the proverbial nose was already in the proverbial tent. In that regard, the zoning history of the Lower East demonstrates the primary challenge to zoning—that of precedent. If a use not allowed by an ordinance predates the ordinance itself, then the prohibition of further instances of that use is, while perhaps legally justified, politically challenging. And once one exception (i.e., variance) is granted, well then…

Perhaps the best example of how dramatic an impact the variances could have is found in that granted for the construction in 1930 of the Brown Motors Building at 200 East. First and foremost, the structure was *large*: twenty-seven thousand square feet, housing an automobile showroom and shops. (Its footprint was larger than that of either the Covey or Buckingham Apartments across the street.) More significant, however, was its design. The new building was a statement of "Modernism, industrially and artistically." Designed by the respected Salt Lake architectural firm Pope and Burton, the Art Deco structure was thoroughly modern from its "modernistic chandeliers with frosted glass" to the "monolithic motif" of the showroom to the façade, which was "highly ornamented with black fluted concrete and aluminum leaf with an extended concrete ornament across the building front."[77]

Unfortunately, the future of Brown Motors was not nearly as bright as that of its showroom. In 1932, Brown Motors lost its franchise for Willys-Knight, along with a significant portion of its inventory. Only two years into its tenancy at 200 East, Brown Motors packed up and moved from the building constructed specifically for it to a new location on Motor Avenue.

The departure of Brown Motors from the sparkling new building did not, however, leave a lingering vacancy. In a prescient move, the property's owner, Zions Securities, had obtained yet another variance—this one to allow it to house a grocery store. The new market, opulently named the "Crystal Palace," was actually the third in what was a rapidly growing chain. So confident was its owner, Verne McCullough, in the franchise that he signed a ten-year lease for the building with Zions Securities. Unfortunately, McCullough's sense of opportunity—at least for that location—appears to

The storefront of the Crystal Palace Market was as opulent as its name, but the building itself would never establish a clear identity. *Utah State Historical Society.*

have been somewhat inflated. Within five years, he had downsized, eventually vacating the store on the corner of 200 East and South Temple, even as he added more locations elsewhere.

With McCullough's departure, the building at 200 East would, over the next ten years or so, witness a veritable parade of transitory tenants: two auto dealerships, the Utah chapter of the USO, a photo studio, a charm school, a modeling agency, various physicians, a "medical center," a purveyor of loans and a "School of Rehabilitation" that promised to help its students "relieve nervous tension and acquire balance and poise" as a means to "correct any weight problem that keeps you from enjoying a healthy vital body."[78] So muddled had the building's use become by 1950 that its two primary tenants were engaged in bottling and auto repair, respectively. The grand structure, once touted as the future of commercial design, had, in only twenty years, completely lost its commercial identity.

It's probable that the building would have plodded on in obscurity had it not been for one of Salt Lake's most enterprising merchants, Samuel Makoff.

His women's department store was, by the early 1950s, a Salt Lake icon—so much so that Makoff needed to move the store from its cramped location in the Medical Arts Building.

So he went prospecting for potential locations farther east on South Temple and in 1951 purchased a lot on the northeast corner of South Temple and A Street, just across from the Brown Motors Building. Although Makoff played his cards close to the vest, insisting that he had no immediate plans for the property, the purchase fueled speculation that he might be planning a new building.

The answer would emerge three years later with the opening of what would be called Makoff's "Fashion Center" on the site of the Brown Motors Building. (Although at the time the property was owned by Zions Securities, Makoff would acquire it several years later.) A retrospective ten years later characterized the business community's response to Makoff's decision to relocate as decidedly skeptical: "'You're out of your mind, Sam' said some knowing businessmen. 'Too far away from the downtown shopping center—a full two blocks.'"[79]

Whether Makoff originally intended to build his new store on the lot on the north side of South Temple is unclear. What he did do, however, was to retain the structure of the Brown Motors Building while modernizing both the interior and exterior. Designed by Ashton, Evans and Brazier, the remodel's cost was, by any standard, extravagant. Estimates at the time ranged from $1 million to nearly $2 million—anywhere from $9 million to over $16 million in 2015 dollars.

The grand opening in 1955 of the Makoff Fashion Center was, indeed, a grand affair, with Salt Lake mayor Earl J. Glade performing the ceremonial ribbon cutting. Opening-day business was brisk, with thousands of people attending the two-hour open house. According to the *Salt Lake Tribune*, "Cars were lined up for six blocks in either direction."[80]

Modern and glamorous as it may have been, the Fashion Center wasn't modern enough. At least, not for the Makoffs themselves. (Makoff's sons were now involved in management of the company.) In 1962, just a few short years after the first remodel, they engaged the services of John Sugden, arguably Utah's most Modernist architect, to redesign the exterior. Not surprisingly, Sugden's vision was about as far removed from the original design as one could get—so much so that it was, for some observers, downright perplexing. In a space of only six months, the *Salt Lake Tribune* alternately referred to the new concept as both a "swank exterior"[81] and a "pretty new bonnet."[82]

Sugden's design was, by South Temple standards, downright avant-garde. The *new* new Makoff was a sleek box set on a pedestal of cast stone impregnated with white quartz. Vertical aluminum mullions framed sheets of black glass. Gone was the grand arched façade of the Crystal Market. Gone were the fluted concrete and aluminum leaf. Gone were all traces of Art Deco flair. The design made an explicit statement that Makoff was, if nothing else, a Modern (with a capital *M*) store. Writing twenty years later, Jack Goodman remarked, "Unless I'm mistaken, Makoff's was the forerunner of the long-lived trend to black-glass exteriors—one of the first 'black boxes' to grace, or, some say, disgrace the Salt Lake City scene." Nevertheless, Goodman added, the remodel represented "a local architectural innovation."[83]

The evolution of the Brown Motors–Makoff Building is instructive, for it distills the broader evolution of the Lower East. In the relatively brief span of only thirty-five years, the building had cycled through numerous uses and guises, struggling to find an identity. Makoff's occupancy in the mid-1950s suggested a glimmer of hope that the property—and the area surrounding it—would find a stable identity. "It [Makoff] will represent establishment of a fashion center with suburban service in a downtown area [drive-in parking]," observed the *Salt Lake Tribune*, "[a]nd the location will mark a trend along East South Temple for other fashion line shops."[84] More than ten years later, that hope still glimmered. "'Fifth Avenue' Moving to E. South Temple," proclaimed the *Tribune*, announcing the relocation of several upscale apparel stores to the Lower East.[85]

But the commercialization of "E. South Temple" was complex and ungainly and, in the end, not nearly as elegant as the community would have liked. To be sure, the Lower East didn't degenerate into a strip of "hamburger and hot dog stands and other undesirable enterprises." But it didn't blossom into Fifth Avenue either. Rather, the commercialization of the Lower East, after the grand debut of the elaborate Brown Motors Building, settled into a progression of relatively modest commercial structures.

Although the *Salt Lake Telegram*'s ominous vision for the rezoning of the Lower East didn't materialize, it's fitting that the first building constructed under the new ordinance was, if not a hamburger or hot dog joint, at least close enough in function to justify some anxiety among those who opposed the new ordinance. In 1935, C.R. Snelgrove was granted permission to erect a building at 224 East South Temple to sell, of all things, ice cream. It was a rather inauspicious beginning for the Lower East's new, open era of commercialization.

While the new ice cream parlor at 224 East was somewhat innocuous, a very different type of commercial intrusion would have a far more insidious impact on the landscape of the Lower East in the years immediately following the 1935 zoning change. Coming as it did at the end of the ordinance's list of newly allowed uses, "gasoline service stations" may have seemed like an afterthought. But at the time the Lower East was rezoned in 1935, there were already several service stations along South Temple. Utah's infatuation with the automobile was only going to intensify and so, too, would the demand for gasoline, tires and auto repair.

So it's not surprising that the most common change in use in the Lower East was to service stations. Between 1935 and 1940, three were constructed: at 302 East, 404 East and 480 East. Although service stations in the Lower East would eventually represent only a handful of all the properties, they would have a disproportionate impact on the landscape because of one key shared attribute: they all occupied corner lots. As a result, they were visually more prominent than they would have been had they been located mid-block.

The primary visual shortcoming of service stations was that they *weren't* visual—that is, they were blank spaces. In appearance, they were closer to vacant lots than to buildings. As a result, certain corners of the Lower East further confused its already disparate identity. This wasn't blight, per se. Generally, the stations were well maintained and reasonably orderly in appearance. But visually and functionally they were so different that they stood in stark relief against the properties around them.

One of those service stations, Standard Oil on the southwest corner of 500 East and South Temple, was part of what might very well have been Salt Lake's first strip mall. Developed in 1935 by Clarence Bamberger, the mall was a low-slung affair that wrapped around the west and south sides of the lot, leaving the middle open for parking and, of course, gas pumps.

For nearly forty years, however, the property had been the site of a very different structure, a three-story, Shingle-style Victorian mansion built for Richard Mackintosh, a Utah mining magnate and one-time president of the Alta Club. When the property was purchased by Bamberger Investment in 1926, Clarence Bamberger informed local papers that he planned to remodel the mansion as a residence for his family. He was true to his word. The Bambergers lived at 474 East for about five years before the home was converted into a reception center called the Cobblemore Town House. For a brief period, the Cobblemore hosted a variety of events—family reunions, banquets and various club meetings.

Built for mining magnate Richard Mackintosh, this grand Victorian home gave way to an unassuming commercial development. *Utah State Historical Society.*

But the fact that the property had been purchased by an investment company, along with Bamberger's admission at the time that "the purchase was largely a matter of investment,"[86] foreshadowed a bleak future for the reception center and, more to the point, for the building itself. In 1934, Richard Mackintosh's grand mansion was demolished to make way for Bamberger Investment's humble strip mall.

While the new commercial building lacked panache, it nevertheless had certain aspirations, as evidenced by the name of its primary tenants: Success Market and Success Pharmacy. Over the years, the strip mall (which itself bore no name) was home to some of Salt Lake's most distinctively named businesses, including Do Ur Shop'n Food Center, Top Hat Flowers, Beauty Box and Seagull Bakery.

Bamberger Investment was clearly opportunistic, developing the site as it did right on the heels of the 1935 zoning change. Clarence Bamberger himself had, in fact, been one of several South Temple property owners who petitioned the City Commission to allow commercial development in the Lower East. Modest as it was, however, the strip mall significantly altered the balance in the Lower East. In 1935, there were only seven commercial enterprises; the Bamberger development alone added four.

In 1935, this corner of 500 East and South Temple turned into what was likely Salt Lake's first strip mall. *Appraisal Card number 2-3315; Box number 108; Tax Appraisal Cards, 1934–1970s; Salt Lake County Assessor; Salt Lake County Records Management & Archives, West Valley City, Utah.*

But it did not prompt a rush of similar developments. In fact, the next ten years saw only a gradual progression of individual commercial buildings, small in scale and simple in design. The first of these might have gone entirely unnoticed, tucked away as it was in the rear of a vacant lot between 200 East and 300 East. The location made perfect sense, however, for the new building constructed in 1938 next to Larkin Mortuary would house Utah's preeminent gravestone manufacturer.

Founded in 1862, Elias Morris & Sons had produced the stonework for many of Salt Lake's most significant buildings, but it was likely better known for its monuments. Its former location at 21 West South Temple, directly across from Temple Square, had been filled with gravestones of various shapes and sizes. For a company as steeped in tradition as Morris & Sons, the new building was, albeit small, surprisingly modern in styling. Its façade was smooth and asymmetrical with a large rectangular window of glass block at its east end. The entrance stood just to the left of center, framed in stone (naturally) and set off by modern aluminum windows. But Morris & Sons' new home was far less permanent than its work. In the early 1960s, it would move to a different location with even more space at 2200 South 700 East. The South Temple office was demolished in the early 1970s to create parking for Larkin Mortuary.

Not all the commercial buildings in the Lower East were new. Two blocks to the east of the venerable Salt Lake institutions of Elias Morris & Sons and Larkin Mortuary, Ella Kelly converted her residence into what was to become the home for another Salt Lake institution. The new building, completed in 1941, was actually two store spaces joined by a single storefront extending across two addresses: 432 East and 434 East. The structure was tiny—only 1,800 square feet in total. But it's what Kelly *didn't* do that might have been as significant as what she *did* do. She didn't demolish the home at 434 East to which the new storefront was affixed. Eventually, the home would be incorporated into the business operations of Kelly's first (and only) tenant at 434 East: Backer's Bakery. For the time being, it would continue to serve as a residence.

Even though commercialization was intensifying in the Lower East, some businesses still did not fit within the parameters of the 1935 ordinance. So it was that Gerhard Backer had to gin up a creative proposition that would circumvent a prohibition of bakeries in the Lower East. He simply changed the nature of the business. "A place where cakes are concocted and decorated isn't a bakery as long as it operates under a restaurant license, the Salt Lake City commission discovered Tuesday," reported the *Salt Lake Tribune*. "Whereupon it granted a tea room license to Gerhard Backer at 434 East South Temple Street."[87] The key distinction, according to the *Tribune*, was that, while bakeries were not permitted by ordinance, tearooms or cafés were, even if they baked their own pastries.

While Backer's Bakery settled in to become a Salt Lake institution (as of this writing, it is still operating out of the storefront at 434 East), the process by which it gained zoning approval is enlightening. The expansion of allowable uses often happens, as in the case of Gerhard Backer's application, by degree—as well as through a certain level of creativity. Backer's concession to the City Commission? That he wouldn't bake bread or engage in any wholesale business. But there was likely no question in the minds of the commissioners that Backer's "tearoom" would really be a front for a bakery.

At the same time that Ella Kelly converted her property to commercial use, Ellen Taylor did the same with her property two blocks to the west. Unlike Kelly, Taylor demolished an existing home to make way for a plain one-story cinder block structure. Like Kelly's, Taylor's building would be small—about 1,500 square feet—and would present two storefronts. Over the years, Taylor's rather undramatic building would be occupied by a series of businesses, including a drapery store, an apparel store, a gift shop, a shoe store and a purveyor of wigs. In the late 1960s, it was purchased by Ben Noda and transformed into Hibachi Restaurant.

Gerhard Backer had to creatively circumvent the zoning ordinance in order to locate his bakery in the Lower East. *Utah State Historical Society*.

As evidenced in particular by Kelly's and Taylor's conversions, commercial developments in the years following the passage of the 1935 zoning ordinance had been small both in number and in scale. The appearance of yet another diminutive, unpretentious building at the corner of 400 East and South Temple in 1941 seemed only to perpetuate that pattern. However, its modest size and appearance belied its potential impact, for it represented the appearance in the Lower East of a new kind of developer: the outside corporate entity. Up to this point, the commercial buildings in the Lower East had all been developed by Salt Lake interests—most of which were simply private individuals. But the new grocery store at 380 East would be constructed by a rapidly growing national chain.

Safeway Stores was the product of a merger in 1926 between a chain of groceries owned by Idaho entrepreneur M.B. Skaggs and Safeway. The consolidated company, which operated a chain of over seven hundred stores, began to engage in an exponential expansion in the 1930s. Several stores

This Safeway store on Main Street in Salt Lake was typical of those being built in the 1940s when a new one appeared at 370 East South Temple. *Utah State Historical Society.*

would be built in Salt Lake, including one on the southwest corner of South Temple and 400 East in 1941.

While the company itself may have been large in size, its stores decidedly were not. They were nothing like the "super" markets that would eventually emerge as commercial development suburbanized. The store at 380 East was typical of those being built in Salt Lake—only about five thousand square feet. (Contemporary supermarkets, by contrast, are often more than ten times that size.) Nevertheless, with a flair for understatement, Safeway touted the new store as "streamlined."

Diminutive as the new Safeway store might have been, it signaled the potential intensification of commercial development in the Lower East. After all, Safeway was a huge, rapidly expanding corporate entity. Its choice to locate along South Temple Street could have sent a signal that the area was now (as the chamber of commerce is inclined to pronounce) "open for business." Corporate capital, especially out-of-state corporate capital, might quite naturally have followed Safeway's example, profoundly altering the character of the Lower East.

But it simply didn't happen. In fact, the grand opening of the Safeway in 1941 represented something like the grand closing of the Lower East. Between 1935 and 1941—the six years since the zoning amendment had opened to commercial development—only a handful of new commercial buildings had been constructed (although, in the process, several homes had been demolished). Over the next ten years, however, the number of new commercial buildings in the Lower East would reach a grand total of…zero.

The reason for the hiatus was simple. America had entered World War II, and the war effort would consume materials—especially the kinds used to construct buildings. The dearth of materials lingered in the years immediately following the war. (Doxey-Layton Realty's expansive plan to construct a new medical building at the corner of 500 East and South Temple was deferred for several years, and the building was ultimately downsized due to a lack of materials.)

Whether the diversion of materials saved the Lower East from more intensive commercialization is hard to say. But even as the materials scarcity of the 1940s diminished, the focus of commercial development energy (and money) was being directed elsewhere: the suburbs. Perhaps the Lower East might still have represented a potentially lucrative location, but the retail markets had shifted significantly. Corporate retailers—department stores, specialty stores and grocery stores—were following the population, which was moving into burgeoning communities out in the valley, some of which had barely existed before the war.

After World War II, only two new retail buildings would be built in the Lower East, both by local companies: Arent's and Felt-Buchorn. As in the Mansion District to the east, the focus of development would shift to corporate interests that wanted to locate offices—not stores—along South Temple. Appropriately, the first new building constructed in the Lower East after World War II presaged this transition.

In 1951, Western Dental Supply moved from the Judge Building at 300 South Main Street to its new offices at 230 East South Temple. Neither the move nor the new building attracted any attention. They shouldn't have. With a specialized market, Western Dental had little reason to promote a "grand opening." And the building itself was modest, standing one story with simple, clean lines. Although the building was likely used to make sales, its primary use was as office space.

As something of a hybrid between retail and corporate space, the Western Dental Building foreshadowed a shift in new development in the Lower East from the former to the latter. So it was that only a year later, the first building in the Lower East used exclusively for offices would appear just a block to the east. This new building would provide a permanent headquarters for the Utah Education Association (UEA), which, since its incorporation in 1910, had been something of an itinerant organization, housed variously in the state capitol, the Beneficial Life Building (aka the Vermont Building) and the Heber J. Grant Building on Main Street.

As early as 1928, UEA had contemplated purchasing its own headquarters, but the idea had stalled during the Great Depression and World War II. Following the war, UEA's programs expanded, but its office space did not. Moving to the Heber J. Grant Building in 1949 did not address the organization's crowded conditions. So, in the early 1950s, UEA began an intensive search for suitable space.

The best site, as it turned out, was at 310 East South Temple Street, because it could "accommodate a building large enough to serve the Association for many years and still provide ample space for parking."[88] The site was also close to the capitol, providing easy access for lobbying. In 1949, UEA purchased the property and promptly demolished an existing home. But construction of its new building was delayed for two years due to limited availability of building materials. Finally, in 1952, nearly twenty-five years after first assessing the viability of a building of its own, UEA broke ground for a new headquarters.

With its completion in 1953, the new UEA headquarters would set a distinctly Modernist tone for the Lower East. Designed by Lowell Parrish, who (appropriately) was forging a career on designing education buildings, the UEA Building featured straight lines with hard edges. Its façade on South Temple was almost entirely glass, framed in the most modern of materials: aluminum. The Utah Education Association sign, in sleek modern (aluminum) lettering, extended along the roofline. On its west side, a bank of windows was accentuated and shaded by an aluminum *bris de soleil*. But perhaps its most striking feature was a set of windows on its northwest and most visible corner that extended the full two stories, from the ground to the roof.

It was a bold statement, standing in stark contrast to its neighbors, particularly the Tudor Revival Barbara Worth next door and the Gothic/Romanesque Cathedral of the Madeleine across the street. But a bold statement was probably just what UEA was seeking, for the building represented a milestone for the organization. Its members had literally earned the right to make a statement, because they had both financed the headquarters (through a special dues assessment) and participated in its design. So proud was UEA president Harold M. Peterson of the yet-to-be-

Completed in 1953, the new headquarters for the Utah Education Association introduced bold Modernist architectural concepts to the Lower East. *Appraisal Card number 2-3335; Box number 108; Tax Appraisal Cards, 1934–1970s; Salt Lake County Assessor; Salt Lake County Records Management & Archives, West Valley City, Utah.*

completed headquarters that in his October 1952 report to UEA's House of Delegates he veered into the evangelical, extolling the building as "your home, your building, your testimony."[89]

The UEA Building signaled an architectural shift in the Lower East. Modernism now had a foothold. This change would manifest itself in ways both dramatic and subtle, further diversifying what had already become an area of diverse architectural styles. Certainly the word "subtle" fit the next in line of the Lower East's Modernist structures: the Felt-Buchorn Building. Constructed in 1959, it was, in many ways, a statement of pure Modernist design: a compact white cube with smooth blank walls composed of porcelain steel panels. Four large vertical windows framed in aluminum highlighted the entrance, which was covered with an aluminum canopy.

But a far more dramatic—and significant—manifestation of Modernism's emerging presence in the Lower East would be constructed two years later a block to the west. This new building would also reflect the evolution of Modernist thinking in the United States. Dubbed "New Formalism," the building's style stemmed from a reaction by some in the design community to the austere, even cold personality exuded by Modernist architecture with its smooth, blank surfaces and rectilinear, geometric forms.

The IBM Building displayed the evolution in Modernist architectural thinking toward designs that incorporated more decorative elements. *Utah State Historical Society.*

The New Formalism movement was led by architects Edward Durell Stone, Minoru Yamasaki and Philip Johnson, who sought to temper Modernism's starkness by reintroducing Classical architectural elements. The result was a hybrid architecture of sorts that combined the rectilinear forms and abstraction of Modernism with Classical elements such as symmetry and arches. New Formalism offered a more accessible alternative to Modernism that presented familiar, albeit modified, architectural elements to a public that found pure Modernism too austere.

Completed in 1961, the IBM Building introduced some of these New Formalist elements to South Temple. Designed by Colorado architect James Hunter, who partnered with Salt Lake architect Donald Panushka, its most prominent feature was its rows of white arches, one of New Formalism's most common treatments. The arches themselves were set off by narrow concrete columns that extended the full three stories. In New Formalist fashion, the building's façade was perfectly symmetrical, with the front entry right in the middle of the ground floor. Set on a platform (a plinth), the building seemed to float.

In the progression of Modernism in the Lower East, the IBM Building presented an even more dramatic statement than its earlier counterpart, the UEA Building. As with the UEA Building, the styling of the IBM Building represented an interesting set of design choices for what was a conservative institution. But IBM's goal with the building was to communicate a progressive side to its "Big Blue" conservatism. "The client's request that the building's look reflect his products' advance," wrote Hunter and Associates in a promotional publication, "we hope was met."[90]

The IBM Building was an architectural milestone for the Lower East—really, for South Temple as a whole—in that it validated the presence of Modernism. That fact was not lost on the community. Immediately upon its completion in 1961, it was termed "one of the most striking buildings in Salt Lake."[91] So significant was its grand opening in January 1962 that it attracted a veritable who's who of civic and business leaders, including Governor George Clyde, Salt Lake mayor J. Bracken Lee, executive secretary of the Salt Lake Chamber of Commerce Gus Backman and president of the University of Utah Ray Olpin.

Although the building was all about IBM (even as of this writing, it is referred to as the "IBM Building" though IBM has long since vacated), it actually belonged to AMCO-Utah, a real estate development company based in Portland, Oregon. The relationship between AMCO-Utah and IBM was of a type that was coming into vogue: a developer builds a building for a specific tenant (perhaps even naming the building after the tenant), then rents the building to the tenant, typically through a long-term lease. The same leasing structure would be utilized for the Metropolitan Life and Xerox Buildings farther east on South Temple and for the Kennecott Building to the west.

That lease arrangement—with a twist—would also be utilized in development of the Lower East's next (and tallest) venture into Modernism: the University Club Building at 136 East. For sixty years, the address had been the site of the University Club, an elegant Classical Revival structure that housed the prestigious organization, founded in 1889. Constructed in 1903, the original building had been designed by prominent Utah architect Walter Ware, whose firm, Ware and Treganza, designed the First

For many years the epitome of elegance, the original University Club Building was replaced in 1965 with a Modernist high-rise. *Utah State Historical Society.*

Presbyterian Church at the corner of South Temple and C Street and the Walker mansion at 610 East South Temple at the same time.

As modern office buildings began to rise downtown, however, a corresponding rise in real estate values caused property owners to consider their development options. Among these were the various social clubs, including the University Club's neighbor. "In the 1950s when the policy of razing buildings to make room for modern and more economically productive structures was popular, Alta Club committees were created from time to time to study the desirability of planning for new quarters in some high rise, multi-purpose structure to be built by the club or leased from some other owner."[92]

While the Alta Club didn't act on this proposition, the University Club did. In 1963, it sold the property at 136 East to an investment group with the rather unimaginative name of 136 East South Temple Inc. Its members, comprising almost entirely out-of-state interests, included the principals of Bloomfield Building Industries, a Tennessee-based construction firm that had constructed and leased office and apartment buildings in cities around the country. The leasing arrangement with a twist? Bloomfield Building

The new University Club Building represented a hybrid of Modernist design ideas. *Author's collection.*

Industries would construct a high-rise office building on the site, and 136 East South Temple Inc. would then lease the top two floors back to the University Club.

The new University Club Building was designed by Salt Lake architect Ashley Carpenter, who, at the same time, was elected president of the University Club. Memphis architect Robert Lee Hall collaborated in the design. When it was completed in the fall of 1965, the new building stood twenty-four stories tall—at the time, the tallest commercial building in the Intermountain West.

Carpenter's design represented something of a progression in Modernist thinking—what might be termed "Modernist Eclectic." Its lower façade, the first six stories, took its cues from New Formalism. Arches framed the ground-floor retail storefronts, while perforated concrete screened the next five floors, which held a parking structure. The upper eighteen floors were set back to diminish the visual impact of the building's height. For fifteen floors, the building was more purely Modernist in appearance—with regular rows of small, square windows creating a distinctly geometric appearance. The top three floors were set off with two bands of horizontal windows separated by porcelain spandrels. The exterior—all white—was, according to Carpenter, "fleshed in precast marble chip panels."[93]

Towering as it did over the downtown landscape (and, not coincidentally, over the Alta Club), it struck a majestic figure. At 375 feet, it was a full six stories taller than the recently completed Kennecott Building a block to the west. Quite literally, it accomplished the lofty goals of the University Club: to capitalize on a financial opportunity presented by rising real estate values and to provide "enlarged, modernized club facilities for our long established social group." An added benefit was that women, who for many years had to enter the club through a side door, would now enjoy "elaborate facilities" for the newly formed "University Club Ladies."[94]

In decidedly less dramatic fashion, Marvin and Lynn Arent moved their fur factory and clothing store from 156 West South Temple to a site just east of the University Club Building. The planned construction of the new Civic Auditorium (the "Salt Palace") in the late 1960s had forced the Arents to find a new location. Completed in 1968, the new "Doorway to Fashion" more closely resembled the older, simpler Western Dental and Taylor Buildings than the newer, more elaborate IBM and University Club Buildings. Two stories tall, its horizontal lines were emphasized by a broad white fascia extending along the roofline. Along with the building's asymmetrical façade, contrasting blocks of color and texture—red brick walls; tall, narrow windows; small, white planter boxes—created visual interest. No arches. No patterned concrete. No symmetry. None of New Formalism's showiness. Just rectilinear boxes set off against one another in a restrained, understated fashion. The building's only dramatic flair appeared in its entrance highlighted by large glass panels.

If Arent's Doorway to Fashion suggested that the architecture of the Lower East was trending toward simpler, less elaborate structures, then the ZCMI Auto Center, completed two doors to the east at essentially the same time, was a clear ratification. Constructed on the southwest corner of South Temple and 200 East, the auto center was a low-slung, brown-brick structure with a façade highlighted by broad arches that framed its large display windows. A fascia of white marble chip highlighted the roofline. All in all, however, it was a remarkably unremarkable structure with function, not aesthetics, in mind.

With the auto center as an apt architectural metaphor, development in the Lower East hit an ebb. For the next seven years, until 1975, only one new building appeared along the street. The reasons for this hiatus are unclear. Perhaps developers were increasingly sensitive to the intensifying outcry about what was happening to South Temple's historic character. Perhaps they were drawn to other places—the suburbs, where commercial development was in full swing, or downtown, where *re*development was in full swing. Whatever the reason, only one building would be constructed between 1968 and 1975: the Chevrolet Building at 303 East.

The property had seen a varied past. For years it was the site of a "fanciful Victorian caricature of mansion proportions" with a grand front porch that overlooked South Temple.[95] The mansion was home, most notably, to John Daly, one of the richest of South Temple's mining magnates. By the 1930s, however, it had been converted to apartments. Eventually, it would hold as many as nineteen. (In a masterful understatement, Hogle Investment at one point advertised it as an investment property with nineteen "small" apartments.)[96]

In 1960, the "caricature" was demolished. The property then went through a series of rapid ownership changes, eventually ending up in the hands of Douglas and Blanche Miles, whose company, Gull Incorporated, would obtain a variance in 1974 to develop the vacant lot. The resulting "Chevrolet Building" was named in honor of its primary tenant and projected from the hillside in dramatic cantilever fashion. Its South Temple façade was defined by tall windows framed by narrow concrete columns. The Chevrolet Building's visual presence belied its relatively small size—only ten thousand square feet in total.

Located at the northwest corner of 500 East and South Temple for over forty years, the Brigham St. Pharmacy was modernized in 1949. *Utah State Historical Society.*

The Chevrolet Building was the last in a line of new commercial buildings in the Lower East, but the Lower East's commercial character was being influenced, as well, by the remodeling—the "modernization"—of a number of buildings. While the Makoff building—in its various iterations—may have represented the most dramatic "makeover," several others, in their own subtler way, contributed to the increasingly commercial character of the Lower East.

The first of these belonged, quite appropriately, to the Lower East's earliest commercial business, the Brigham St. Pharmacy, which had been John Sharp's first tenant. With the pharmacy having reached the ripe old age of forty in 1949, its owner, Christopher Athas, decided that it was time for a facelift. The remodel transformed the storefront with contemporary finishes: dark marble panels along the storefront, a contrasting band of stucco above and a bold sign with an Art Deco flair. (Athas also converted the use of the upper floors from apartments to medical offices.)

The "face lifting" (as the *Salt Lake Tribune* characterized it) was a big deal—such a big deal that it prompted Athas to hold a "formal reopening" in June 1949. Lest potential customers think that he had simply refashioned a stodgy old drugstore, Athas took out a full-page ad in the *Salt Lake Tribune* that featured the word "modern" no fewer than five times—even boasting that the new and (of course) modern fountain was "sparkling" with "every new innovation."[97]

Athas's remodel certainly contemporized the character of John Sharp's building. But the makeover completed by George Q. Morris several years later took another historic building and completely transformed it into a bold Modernist statement. Morris, the owner of Morris Monuments, had purchased the modest home at 242 East in 1945. Perhaps inspired by the extensive use of glass in the UEA Building a half block to the east, Morris added a storefront almost entirely of glass, exposing the building (and its merchandise) to the street. Above the storefront rose a sleek, black cube. Behind, the house itself was literally boxed in. To passersby, the building presented three distinct cubes of material and color.

Unlike Athas's and Morris's projects, the last of the Lower East's makeovers did not affect the original building. Rather, separate structures—wings—were added that significantly altered its appearance without altering *it*. That building, the Enos Wall mansion at 411 East, was one of the grandest in the parade of grand South Temple mansions.

In 1904, Wall purchased the property, hired noted Utah architect Richard Kletting and spent $300,000 (over $8 million in 2015 dollars) to transform an existing adobe home (that was itself rather elaborate) into a "palatial dwelling resembling a Renaissance villa."[98] Wall died in 1920; his widow, Mary, died in 1923. Three years later, the property was sold for literally pennies on the dollar to a group of Jewish investors who converted the mansion into the Jewish Community Center. The result was that the mansion's use would forever change.

The Jewish Community Center (JCC) called the Wall mansion home for twenty-five years. While it made some modifications to the interior of the building, it left the exterior essentially unchanged. In 1950, the JCC sold the property to Pacific National Life Assurance for essentially the same price that it had paid: $100,000. (By this time, the property had been devalued by about 90 percent from Wall's original investment.)

In September 1950, Pacific National Life Assurance occupied its new home on South Temple. Even before the move, however, the company had plans to modify the mansion. The interior was remodeled (again) "to form an efficient office unit," and a wing was constructed on the mansion's west side "to accommodate operations of the insurance firm."[99] Designed by

The Wall mansion, built in 1911, became home to Pacific National Life Assurance in 1950. *Utah State Historical Society.*

Lorenzo Snow Young, the wing didn't resemble a corporate office so much as a school—not surprising, since Young was entering a period in which he would design (among others) Evergreen Junior High School, Olympus High School and Highland High School.

The building was a low, horizontal structure—Modernist in its rectangular profile. Its south end—facing South Temple—was notably blank, with just a single two-story panel of windows. The walls were covered in a smooth precast architectural stone. Whatever Young's instructions from his clients, the visual impact of the wing was remarkably understated. Nevertheless, it was deceptively large, adding fourteen thousand square feet of office space to Pacific National Life's headquarters. Young's firm would later design a second wing for the property's new owners, the LDS Business College. Like the earlier addition, the new wing would be two stories tall. It, too, would be larger than it appeared, adding thirteen thousand square feet of space to the college.

The two additions, built years apart, were essentially twins. But their achievement was that, at the same time they created additional space, they

Over time, wings were constructed on either side of the Wall mansion. The first one was completed in 1950 to provide additional office space for Pacific National Life. *Appraisal Card number 09-31-458-007; Box numbers 15B; Tax Appraisal Cards, 1934–1970s; Salt Lake County Assessor; Salt Lake County Records Management & Archives, West Valley City, Utah.*

did not detract from the visual impact of the Wall mansion itself. Because they were so different from the mansion—in size, in profile, in style—they, in many ways, enhanced its presence by setting it off.

By the time the second wing was completed in 1975, the Lower East was a very different place than it had been only fifty years earlier. Buildings of varying sizes, styles and uses populated what could only be termed an eclectic landscape. Yet even with so much diversity, that landscape—and the very character of the Lower East—was influenced as much by what *didn't* happen as by what did. All told, at least nine major concepts never materialized. Had things gone differently, the west end of the Lower East might have transformed into the "radio district." An extravagant arts center would have stood at 200 East. And South Temple would have boasted the city's premier miniature golf course. These proposed projects were often highly publicized. But their disappearance was veiled and mysterious, treated as if the original concept had never existed.

The most ambitious of these (certainly the largest) was a 1951 proposal to construct a twenty-two-story apartment and office building on the northeast corner of South Temple and A Streets. It would have been a massive structure—at that time the tallest in the city, towering 225 feet and extending 100 feet along South Temple. A 900-stall parking structure would have sat beneath it. It would have contained 250 offices, 50 apartments and studios for both radio and television. Each apartment would have had its own terrace, making all the apartments "of the penthouse type." The building's tower was "designed as an observation post for tourists and others" that would have provided "a view which will be blocked only by the mountains" (which, presumably, weren't themselves worthy of viewing).[100] In a fit of hubris, its developers envisioned it as "Radio City Salt Lake."

Groundbreaking for Radio City Salt Lake was set for October 1951. But no ground was broken. As with other projects that died on the vine, there was no public post-mortem. The grand tower, garden apartments and radio studios silently and secretively drifted into the ether. However, some clues as to the dissolution of Radio City Salt Lake may lie in various newspaper accounts. Initially, the total cost was estimated at $8 million (about $73 million in 2015 dollars), but within months that figure had skyrocketed to close to $12 million (nearly $110 million in 2015 dollars). As the concept was rolled out, the *Salt Lake Tribune* made the rather murky observation that "the contractors conceded several obstacles still stood in the path of their project."[101]

But interest in the site did not wane. Twelve years later, Artcol, a California-based developer, signed a fifty-five-year lease with Zions Securities (which had purchased the property in 1960) to construct an apartment building—the Plaza Tower—on that corner. Artcol's development agenda was aggressive, for it was about to launch construction of two other large apartment buildings: the Sunset Tower at 40 South 900 East and Bonneville Tower at 777 East South Temple.

While those buildings were completed by 1965, ground at the corner of South Temple and A Streets remained undisturbed. Artcol had encountered financial difficulties, building too many apartment units too fast in a city in which too many apartment units were already being built too fast. In 1966, the Federal Housing Administration foreclosed on Bonneville and Sunset Towers. The anticipated financing for the Plaza Tower—which, most likely, would have looked much like its siblings—would not be forthcoming.

At this point, it should have seemed to even the most optimistic of developers that the site carried some sort of curse. Yet even after two failed development proposals, the site's appeal still lingered. In 1972, Empire West received a variance from the Board of Adjustment to construct yet another apartment building. The permit was granted, but Empire West quietly withdrew its application a month later—so quietly that neither the approval nor the withdrawal received mention in local newspapers.

The "Radio City" concept, however grand, wasn't necessarily new. Several years earlier, KUTA had envisioned a similarly grand edifice on

South Temple. Founded in 1938, KUTA had initially operated out of the Belvedere Apartment Hotel near the corner of State Street and South Temple. In 1944, its parent company, Utah Broadcasting, had purchased properties at 201 East and 217 East with the pronouncement that it would construct a "substantial two-story structure housing four large studios, an auditorium, F-M and television facilities."[102] The proposed building almost immediately grew to three stories. All that stood in the way was a lack of materials. "Construction will begin immediately after materials become available," station co-owner Frank Carman told the *Salt Lake Tribune*. "With the present news of war developments," Carman continued, "ground may be broken this year."[103]

Carman's optimism was amplified by the final, exuberant design, prepared by Pope and Thomas. Known as the "KUTA Radio Center," the proposed building stretched over two hundred feet along South Temple, and its bands of ribbon windows were set off by lines of straight awnings that accentuated its horizontality. Its entrance was embellished by a graceful curved canopy juxtaposed against the rectilinear form of the building itself. But its most distinctive feature was a massive tower projecting five stories from its southwest corner with K-U-T-A boldly spelled out vertically in one-story-tall letters.

Once again, however, ground wasn't broken (although a home at 201 East was demolished). As with the various proposals for the northeast corner of South Temple and A Streets, the KUTA Radio Center concept faded into the mists of obscurity. Again, the reasons for its demise are now matters of conjecture. But in 1951, the principals in Utah Broadcasting sold the property to Thorpe Isaacson who, in turn, would sell it to Makoff Realty, which would use it as a parking lot for the Makoff store across the street.

These proposals envisioned large, bold projects that would have dramatically altered the landscape of the Lower East. Ironically, their absence created as dramatic an impact as their presence might have. With no buildings occupying them, the various properties languished as vast expanses of nothing. From the Elks Building on the west to the Covey Apartments on the east—basically a full block—the only structure standing after 1945 was the Knights of Columbus home at 165 East. Nearly half of the space along South Temple's north side between State and A Streets was empty.

Perhaps the owners of these properties might have taken their cue from florist Uhra Huff to find a viable use for relatively flat vacant ground. In 1930, Huff had applied for and was granted permission to construct a miniature golf course on the corner of South Temple and 300 East. Why would a professional florist, of all people, want to build a miniature golf course? The answer was simple: Huff was an avid golfer who competed regularly in local tournaments. In 1934, she, quite naturally, won the putting prize in a municipal golf tournament. Avid as she might have been, however, she, like the large corporations with their grand ideas, did not break ground. The property at the southeast corner of South Temple and 300 East would eventually be developed as a service station.

In its own personal way, Huff's golf course was a grand idea. But among the grand ideas for development in the Lower East that died prematurely, none may have been as architecturally elaborate yet as absolutely unrealized as that proposed for the "top" of 200 East. Had it been constructed, it would have upped the ante of Modernist architecture in the Lower East—well beyond that standard set by the UEA Building or the IBM Building or even George Q. Morris's abstract remodel.

In 1962, a coalition of civic leaders presented Salt Lake City with the expansively titled "Second Century Plan" that articulated a whole host of big ideas directed at launching the city into its next one hundred years. Among these was the concept to construct a community arts center on the north side of South Temple at its intersection with 200 East. (The site in question included the property that might have been occupied by KUTA Radio Center.) "The proposed location at the head of Second East Street," stated the plan, "will form a magnificent focus and will strengthen the existing character of South Temple."[104]

The plan even offered a detailed rendering of the center, an eclectic campus of buildings in the shape of a *U*. A distinctly New Formalist structure with a colonnade of tall arches formed the base, from which two rectangular buildings extended into pavilions with canopies supported by mushroom pillars à la Frank Lloyd Wright. "The center of the structure," suggested the plan, "could be opened for gardens to tie into the historically significant grave of Brigham Young on the hill above."[105] But the arts center with its arches and mushroom pillars and gardens never left the page, despite the fact that—at least in the mind of the artist who created the drawing—it was a fully developed idea.

There were, of course, other "fully developed" ideas for development in the Lower East that never left the minds of *their* creators. Some simply never materialized. Others were denied outright by the Board of Adjustment. Individually, these were much more modest concepts than those presented by the principals in KUTA or the Second Century Plan committee or even by Uhra Huff—a small apartment building here, a modest commercial

Salt Lake's "Second Century Plan," issued in the early 1960s, included a proposal for an elaborate art center "at the head of Second East Street." *University of Utah Marriott Library Special Collections.*

building there, perhaps an addition to an existing building. But cumulatively they demonstrate that a place—in this case, the Lower East—can be affected as profoundly by what *doesn't* happen as by what does.

By 1975, with all that did and didn't happen, the Lower East's identity crisis was even more acute than it had been fifty years earlier. The four blocks that might euphemistically have been characterized as eclectic in 1925 would now more accurately have been characterized as muddled. Single-family residences, which had in 1925 represented nearly half of all the properties, were gone entirely (although some houses remained in other uses). Vacant lots (some passing as parking lots) dominated the landscape. Apartment houses of various sizes, shapes and styles were interspersed. Small commercial buildings huddled in clusters—almost all on the south side of the street. (Even though the north side was designated with the same zoning classification as the south, only two of twenty-four properties on the north side were commercial.) Modernist office buildings appeared intermittently. Even with the adoption of increasingly refined zoning ordinances and the intensifying attention of the community at large, the Lower East had failed to gain a clear sense of self, a clear character.

4

THE MANSION DISTRICT

"Mature Vandalism Masquerading as Progress"

B righam Street" was the name given to the stretch of South Temple that ran east from Temple Square up a long, gentle hill to the neighborhood bordering the area that would grow into the University of Utah. By the turn of the twentieth century, it had become, without question, Salt Lake's most prestigious address, an enclave for Utah's rich and famous. Lined with extravagant mansions, Brigham Street was an almost mythical place:

> *Along the roadway beautifully matched horses pulled Salt Lake City's stylish society. Somewhere on the street of an evening some gala affair would be in progress. Handsome carriages drawing up to the walks revealed ladies in shimmering satins, brocades, velvets, or chiffons with sequins, laces, and ermine.*
>
> *People came to gaze at the enchanting scene and were captivated by the display of wealth and the mode of living. There were lavish balls and extravagant weddings. Names of the wealthy appeared daily in the society news. Entertainments, parties, teas, "at homes," travels abroad, trips to a neighboring city for the weekend—everything was newsworthy.*[106]

Although Brigham Street stretched twelve blocks, its epicenter lay in a three-block area from 500 East to 800 East—the "Mansion District." Here gathered the greatest concentration of extravagant estates belonging to South Temple's wealthiest elite: Cosgriff, Dooly, Hogle, Kearns, Walker, Dern, MacVichie, Jackling and Bonnemort. Their mansions were exhibitions of

SALT LAKE CITY   VIEW ALONG SOUTH TEMPLE ST.
1912   No. 2666

In the words of historian Margaret Lester, in the early 1900s, Brigham Street was "the most beautiful thoroughfare between Denver and San Francisco." *Utah State Historical Society.*

wealth, brash expressions of conspicuous consumption. The designers of this grandeur read like a who's who of Utah architects: Richard Kletting, Carl Neuhausen and Frederick Hale, among others.

The mansions were large, some as big as twenty thousand square feet with as many as thirty rooms. They were lavish, finished in Italian marble, French oak and Russian mahogany. Tiffany glass was everywhere—in lamps, in windows, in skylights. And they were extravagant, sporting bowling alleys, indoor shooting galleries, even an Aeolian pipe organ whose pipes rose three stories. These were palaces that evoked wonder and amazement among the commoners.

By their very mass, Brigham Street's mansions might also have evoked a sense of permanence. In the early 1900s, the average Salt Lake resident would likely have assumed that Brigham Street—the boulevard of grand estates—would last forever. But change was in the air. As historian Margaret Lester described it, for a fictional pedestrian of the period that change would have been almost palpable: "Upon reaching the eastern end of the grand boulevard and pausing to reflect upon the magnificence of his walk, the traveler may well have sensed the twilight of an era."[107]

Quite simply, attrition began to take its toll on Brigham Street. For most of the principals living between 500 East and 800 East, it came in the form of death. By 1925, two-thirds of Brigham Street's progenitors were dead—by 1940, nearly 90 percent. Some of the living chose to move. David and Mary Keith moved to the Hotel Utah in 1916, but both died within three years. Emma McMillan and her son Gordon moved to the Bransford Apartments after the death of Emma's spouse, Henry McMillan. Daniel Jackling moved to San Francisco in 1915. Lottie Dern moved to the East Coast in the late 1930s, following the death of her husband, George. As their owners moved and/or died, the grand mansions inevitably fell into new ownership. And new ownership foretold change.

Twilight was encroaching, as well, on the economic high times that generated the exorbitant incomes that had built Brigham Street. Although World War I created huge demand for Utah's primary exports—metals and foods—its aftermath left the state in an "inventory depression," as the demand abruptly ceased.[108] Mining production plummeted, recovered briefly in the 1920s and then plummeted again with the onset of the Great Depression, which was "catastrophic" for Utah's mining industry, as output fell to half of 1919 levels.[109]

Along with cutbacks in production, whatever profits were generated from Utah's mines were increasingly exported to corporations in other parts of the country. In 1915, for example, Kennecott Copper had purchased a 25 percent interest in the Utah Copper and Boston Consolidated Company. Whatever wealth was coming out of the mines was no longer going to a few individuals who lived along South Temple or even to corporate entities in Salt Lake. It was leaving Utah entirely.

That wealth was going not only to out-of-state corporations, it was also going to Washington, D.C. In 1913, Congress had instituted the first permanent personal income tax. With the onset of World War I, the federal government confronted the need to raise massive amounts of capital to fund the war effort. Tax rates on the super wealthy became almost draconian, rising to over 75 percent. Although the rates moderated somewhat in the 1920s, they were raised again during the Great Depression. The collective impact of these economic changes was dramatic. Between the end of World War I and 1930—less than fifteen years—the number of personal tax returns from Utah in the highest-income brackets dropped by more than 50 percent. Brigham Street was not only losing the people who had built it, it was losing its wealth as well.

The conditions that diminished South Temple's wealth also quite naturally affected its real estate. By 1930, there just weren't many individuals with enough money in Salt Lake to afford the luxurious mansions that were going up for sale. As more estates entered the market, their values declined. Yet they were still priced well outside the reach of the average Utah resident. As early as 1919, the Walker mansion, for example, was listed for the bargain price of $65,000 (nearly $900,000 in 2015 dollars)—less than half of its original cost but still much more than even the upper middle class might afford.

Aside from the gloomy realities of the broader real estate market, the mansions had their own inherent limitations. Built as what historians Thomas Alexander and James Allen characterized as "personal monuments," they expressed the particular, sometimes idiosyncratic, styles and tastes of their owners.[110] Potential buyers would have had to share those styles and tastes. More likely, though, buyers who could have afforded Brigham Street's mansions would have been motivated simply to build their own. After all, wasn't the purpose of a personal monument to create one's *own* expression of conspicuous consumption?

For those who could afford it, Brigham Street was still regarded as a prestigious street. But that title was no longer exclusive. Other areas of the city were coming into vogue: Federal Heights, Harvard-Yale and the upper East Bench. An ad for Bonneville-on-the-Hill boasted in 1919 that "MILITARY WAY IS TO BE IN THE NEAR FUTURE WHAT SOUTH TEMPLE WAS—THE HOME STREET BEAUTIFUL."[111] (Ironically, on the same page of the *Salt Lake Tribune* appeared the ad for the Walker mansion.)

Not all the new havens for the rich and famous were in Salt Lake City. Like other members of Salt Lake's elite, the Walker family built a "country home" out in the valley. On (of course) Walker Lane in Holladay, Glenwood was a mansion lavish enough to have found itself on Brigham Street.

Some of Brigham Street's elite stayed on South Temple but chose to relocate to apartments—smaller, perhaps, but no less extravagant. The Bransford and Mayflower, for example, offered the sumptuous qualities of a mansion (including servants' quarters) without the demands of maintaining a large property. For those who remained, many of Brigham Street's mansions had degenerated to financial burdens, especially as the owners' children grew up and moved out, leaving the parents alone in large, mostly empty spaces. The heirs who inherited the mansions assumed the responsibility of maintaining properties that were no longer their homes and in which they likely had little personal interest.

For the Judge children, for example, their mother's mansion at 737 East devolved into a money pit, as property taxes came to exceed the value of the home. "Old Judge Home Fails to Escape Time and Taxes," mourned the *Salt Lake Tribune* in 1933. "Present owners have found that its decline in value was more rapid than the decline in assessed valuation. Originally estimated to have cost from $35,000 to $50,000 to build the assessor held high the old home's head with a valuation of from $7,500 to $8,000 and by the sheer force of economics it was found better to level the building rather than to pay taxes on any valuation 'out of line' with actual value."[112]

The demise of the Judge mansion demonstrates the dramatic dissolution in value of South Temple's grand estates. And as their monetary value declined, their prestige declined as well. Brigham Street's gold-plated finish was beginning to tarnish. South Temple's allure as *the* residential address was fading.

That process, however, had actually been set into motion years earlier during Brigham Street's heyday near the turn of the century. It was initiated by what might have seemed to the average Salt Lake resident as an improvement—the paving of South Temple. In spite of its seemingly positive impacts, South Temple's residents were divided about the project's benefits. Yet it wasn't the paving that worried opponents. It was the leveling of the street. At an August 1904 city council meeting with a "lively debate" regarding the proposed project, several property owners along South Temple threatened to file suit "if the grade of the street is lowered as proposed in the plan."[113]

Until 1904, the stretch of South Temple east of State Street—Brigham Street—had been divided. Running as it did west and east along a south-facing slope, Brigham Street had originally been constructed on two levels—essentially two streets—a higher northern east–west lane and a lower southern west–east lane for vehicular traffic. The protesters at the 1904 city council meeting preferred the existing configuration with "a retaining wall, and practically two streets."[114]

However compelling their arguments (and threats of litigation), the protestors did not prevail. The leveling of South Temple proceeded, effectively widening the street and, more significantly, facilitating the flow of traffic. As a result, Brigham Street began to transform from a quiet avenue to a major thoroughfare that, with the advent of the automobile, became increasingly uncomfortable as a place to live. So much so, that by 1928 when the street was designated for repaving, South Temple residents protested again. No less than the governor himself, George Dern (a resident of South Temple), was among those opposing the repaving. The protests were equally strident to

South Temple Street being leveled for paving, 1904. *Utah State Historical Society.*

The automobile pictured here following the leveling and paving of South Temple was an ominous sign portending Brigham Street's transformation into a busy thoroughfare. *Utah State Historical Society.*

those made a quarter of a century earlier. "We do not want a race course made out of South Temple street [*sic*] between E and Virginia streets, to endanger the lives of our children," read one quote in the *Salt Lake Telegram*.[115]

But east South Temple's transformation to a "race course" was as inexorable as Utah's infatuation with the automobile. Utahns, like other Americans, would fall in love with the car. Between 1920 and 1940, the number of cars registered in Utah would grow more than ten times as fast as the state's population. Increasingly, many of those cars would travel on South Temple between Salt Lake's business and academic centers: downtown and the University of Utah.

However, cars would also induce a different but no less subtle change along South Temple. Together with leveling and paving, parking would profoundly alter the landscape of east South Temple, as the new property owners—corporations, developers and social institutions—confronted an increasing demand for parking space from their employees, clients, members and visitors.

Cumulatively, biology, economics and the automobile were, by 1925, exerting tremendous pressure for change on east South Temple. Nowhere would it be more pronounced than in the three-block stretch between 500 East and 800 East. Brigham Street's epicenter—the several blocks of stately mansions and large estates—would transform from a quiet enclave of grand mansions into a busy district of corporate offices, medical offices and social/fraternal clubhouses.

Yet the first new building would have seemed at the time only to reinforce the status quo. Although its use was substantially different than that of its mansion neighbors, the Masonic temple at 650 East carried on Brigham Street's tradition of architectural ornamentation and extravagance. Designed by noted Utah architect Carl Scott in the Egyptian Revival style, it presented seemingly all manner of symbolic references, most notably matching sphinxes flanking its grand entrance. Different in scale and use, the Masonic temple nevertheless shared two key qualities with its mansion neighbors: it was extremely large and exceedingly ornate.

But certain aspects of the construction of the Masonic temple foreshadowed the more disparate changes that would impact the Mansion District. Because it would be financed with collective capital (that is, a pool of funds gathered by a group of individuals), the funds being raised within the membership of the various Salt Lake Masonic lodges, the construction of the temple signaled the demise of the individual owner in the Mansion District. From now on, the properties along those three blocks would, with few exceptions, be purchased by groups rather than by individuals. Consequently, they would no longer serve as single-family residences.

The temple's construction also portended the demise of various landmarks in the Mansion District. While some of the land purchased for the temple was vacant, one of the several lots that it would occupy was the site of the Chisholm home and stable. Characterized by the *Salt Lake Telegram* as a "landmark," it nevertheless "had to give way to the march of improvement." With the demolition, the three lots purchased by the Masons provided ample space—not only for the massive temple but also for parking. As the *Telegram* went on to note, "Special attention will be given to the general design for automobile parking."[116] This new use represented a significant shift in the way in which South Temple's large estates would be viewed. Their appeal now lay not so much in the grand mansions that occupied them but in the space that they afforded for both buildings *and* parking. The mansions might be replaced by office buildings, but the carriage houses and gardens would be replaced by parking lots.

The Masonic temple may have represented something of an architectural throwback, but by the 1930s, new ideas were influencing Utah architects. A reaction to the perceived excesses of the period that had produced Brigham Street's extravagant mansions, these ideas de-emphasized ornament and historical reference in favor of a more subdued, understated expression. Ironically, the first building in a more contemporary style to appear in the Mansion District was designed by none other than Carl Scott, the very same architect who had designed the traditionalist Masonic temple.

In 1937, the Intermountain Clinic opened its new offices at 699 East in what the *Deseret News* termed a "modernistic" structure.[117] Scott's design would be South Temple's only example of Streamline Moderne architecture. Built out of steel, concrete, stucco and brick, the building stood two stories tall and stretched north along I Street. With distinct bands of stucco along its roofline, contrasting brick around its windows and Streamline Moderne's signature curved corners, the clinic introduced South Temple to a new form of elegance, one that offered a much subtler ornamentation than had been exhibited in the street's decorative mansions.

In relocating to South Temple from downtown, the Intermountain Clinic group was almost like a band of contemporary pioneers, moving from the settlement to a place akin to the frontier. So removed was South Temple perceived to be that the partners even had difficulty securing financing, as "bank after bank rejected their request as too risky—too risky to build a professional medical building in a residential area seven blocks east of

The Intermountain Clinic Building introduced early Modernist architectural ideas to the Mansion District with its elegant Moderne style. *Utah State Historical Society.*

downtown, away from all other medical offices. People wouldn't patronize such a medical office that far away from the convenience of the downtown area."[118] Contrary to the banks' perception, the principals were trendsetters, for they would be among the first of many companies that would move away from a downtown that increasingly suffered from traffic congestion and a lack of parking.

The distance between downtown and the frontier of South Temple would shrink considerably over the next forty years, as the Mansion District increasingly came to be viewed as something of an annex, an extension of downtown with both the access to business activity that downtown had traditionally provided and the space for parking that suburban locations now provided. While they likely didn't see themselves as doing so when they built their clinic in 1937, the clinic's partners foreshadowed several important trends in the Mansion District: the introduction of nonresidential uses, the demolition of existing structures to make way for parking and the infiltration of a very different set of architectural ideas.

Elegant as it may have been, the Intermountain Clinic's Streamline Moderne design was revolutionary for the Mansion District. The Moderne style in its various manifestations fused the concepts of the emerging field of industrial design with the principles of Modernism that were finding their way to the United States from Europe. For many Modernists, Moderne was pop architecture, a mainstream derivative of Modernism that lacked the purity and integrity of Modernism's lofty architectural and social ideals. Nevertheless, at a simple aesthetic level Moderne design communicated the same visual ideals found in Modernist designs: geometric forms, smooth surfaces and—most notably—a lack of applied ornament. In its own subtle way, the Intermountain Clinic would introduce Modernism to the Mansion District.

But the first truly Modernist structure in the Mansion District would not appear for more than ten years. First, Utah would have to emerge from the grip of the Great Depression and the hiatus of World War II. As it did, it entered a period of abundant prosperity. Stimulated by intensive defense spending during and following the war, Utah's economy flourished, prompting construction of all types. And the Mansion District, which had languished during the war years, received new interest. But it was not the interest of individuals or families looking to live on South Temple. The attention came from companies, developers and institutions looking to capitalize on the Mansion District's expansive lots.

The motivation of the first of these postwar developers, the Doxey-Layton Realty Company, to build in the Mansion District was made abundantly clear by the *Salt Lake Tribune*, which wrote about the new medical building that company was constructing: "The structure, a multi-story brick building, is one of several being built outside the shopping district of Salt Lake City by various interests. Those associated with such ventures have pointed out that in all cases, *availability of parking space* has been a major factor in the decision as to location."[119] (author's emphasis)

Prompted perhaps by Brigham Street's extravagant past, Doxey-Layton purchased the Dooly property at 508 East with grand plans. Those plans necessitated demolition of the Dooly mansion, an elaborate Victorian structure dating to the 1870s. Although the mansion was considered a landmark, local attitudes about its demolition were very much the same as they were regarding the demolition of other historic buildings. After its purchase by Doxey-Layton in 1945, the mansion had been neglected, so its demise seemed inevitable—at least to the *Salt Lake Tribune*—which noted drily that it "succumbed to the push of progress."[120]

Initially, "progress" was envisioned as a "modernistic apartment house" rising six stories above the street.[121] But the building's concept changed, and by 1947, the plans called for a "modern five or six story, fireproof doctors' office building."[122] The change in use from an apartment building to a medical center, though somewhat abrupt, wasn't unfounded. The years following World War II saw an emerging national healthcare industry stimulated by the increasing availability of health insurance and the return

The Dooly mansion on the corner of 500 East and South Temple was the first of Brigham Street's mansions to be demolished for a Modernist structure. *Utah State Historical Society*.

of so many injured veterans. In addition, the University of Utah's medical school was growing following the hiring in the early 1940s of the first set of full-time faculty members and accreditation in 1944 as a four-year medical school. And new hospitals were being constructed in Salt Lake, including Shriners Hospital and the Veterans Administration Hospital.

Physicians were now in high demand. So, in turn, were physicians' offices. Doxey-Layton's choice to change the use from an apartment building to a medical office building was a natural response to those changes in demand. But other market forces also affected the ultimate design of the building. The high-style, five-story Modernist building originally envisioned would—due to shortages in materials—be significantly scaled back, both in size and in style, to a much more modest, understated three-story brick structure.

With the exception of its stone-framed entryway, it was essentially without ornamentation—even more spare than the Intermountain Clinic. Faced with rose-colored firebrick, it presented rows of "ribbon windows" that wrapped around its corners, emphasizing its horizontal profile. It stood in

The Doxey-Layton Medical Center foreshadowed the shift in use in the Mansion District from extravagant residences to everyday medical and professional offices. *Amanda Moore.*

stark contrast to the elaborate mansion it had replaced, as well as those that still stood around it, thus intensifying the understated Modernist aesthetic that had been introduced by the Intermountain Clinic building.

While the Doxey-Layton Medical Center was introducing dramatic change at the corner of 500 East and South Temple, across the street another medical building was taking a different approach to altering the landscape of the Mansion District. The Callister Clinic at 559 East would be the first example of the "modernization" of an existing building. Built by Ben Eldredge in the 1880s, the home had been purchased in 1937 by Dr. Cyril Callister, a lecturer at the University of Utah School of Medicine. (Callister would become more well known as dean of the School of Medicine, which he would guide through the transition from a two-year to a four-year program.)

Callister appears to have had no immediate plans for the Eldredge home, for he maintained its use as a rental property for the next ten years. In 1949, however, he decided to move from his office in the Medical Arts Building at 54 East South Temple and convert the home to a clinic. In doing so, he transformed Ben Eldredge's multifaceted Victorian home into a sleek Modernist cube—not too dissimilar from the Intermountain Clinic just down the street. A dormer and gable on the front were removed to create a smooth façade; the existing arched, double-hung windows were replaced with rectangular metal casement windows; the roof was leveled; and the exterior walls were painted white. As the *Salt Lake Tribune* remarked twenty-five years later, the Modernist remodel was akin to "shucking off 'grandma's lace collars.'"[123]

Dr. Callister's decision to locate on South Temple was characterized at the time as a sign of "an advancing business district" along the street.[124] What less than fifteen years earlier had been considered to be almost isolated from downtown was now considered prime commercial real estate. South Temple's expansive lots and lack of congestion were becoming increasingly attractive to companies looking to relocate from Salt Lake's congested central business district.

Many companies that fled downtown chose to move to Salt Lake County's rapidly growing suburbs with their emerging markets and readily available land. But some chose to remain close to downtown even as they deserted it. Though downtown may have been in decline, it was still the state's central business district. The Mansion District offered the best of both worlds: the space of the suburbs and the connectedness to Salt Lake's business hub—with the lingering air of prestige.

This practical combination of traits was clearly articulated by Royal W. Gelder as the primary factor in the Tracy Insurance Company's decision to relocate to South Temple in 1957. Writing in the *Northwest Insurance News*, Gelder summarized the company's thought process:

> *Naturally, the first problem was location. Should we locate in downtown Salt Lake City, or perhaps move out into the suburbs? Both locations offer advantages and disadvantages. In the heart of town there is always a traffic problem, and the suburbs are just a little too far from the center of things.*
>
> *We solved this problem by location [sic] just outside the congested area; therefore having the advantages of both suburban and city-center locations, and none of the disadvantages of either.*[125]

The outcome of this selection process was the decision to purchase a property at 780 East South Temple. Once the site of a mansion belonging to rancher Elizabeth Bonnemort, the property had sat vacant since the home's demolition in 1929. Previous owners had submitted several proposals for developing the property—including a gas station, a market, even a theater—all of which had been denied by the Salt Lake Board of Adjustment.

The modest Tracy Insurance Building presented Modernism in its simplest form. *Utah State Historical Society.*

By South Temple's architectural standards, the Tracy Insurance Company's new building was painfully modest. Only one story tall, it presented a plain brick exterior, punctuated in the front with a simple glass entry framed in aluminum. Even the company's sign, perched in the upper left-hand corner of the façade, was understated to the point of being demure.

If it lacked any architectural flair, the Tracy Insurance Building did have one element that was meaningful for the future of the Mansion District: an open floor plan. This new concept was a trend that would increasingly define the "modern" work space. However, it was a trend that didn't bode well for the Mansion District's mansions. Although a few tenants would eventually occupy mansions as office space, the challenge of adapting a large home with as many as thirty rooms to a modern office for dozens of workers was, to say the least, challenging, especially given the popularity of the trendy open floor plan concept. Given the negligible costs of demolition, it would be far less expensive and far more expedient simply to tear down a mansion and construct a new office building in its place. Not surprisingly, the Mansion District would see a flurry of demolitions accompanied by the construction of new office buildings. Within ten years, six new structures would appear, all of which would intensify Modernism's presence along the street at the expense of historic homes and mansions.

These newer buildings would reflect a broader evolution that was occurring in the Modernist movement. As it had developed in the United States, the Modernism imported from Europe—generally perceived as cold and austere—had been adapted to appeal to more traditional mainstream American sensibilities. Particularly on the West Coast, architects had expanded the Modernist palette of steel, glass and concrete to include natural materials such as stone, marble and wood. Even concrete was manipulated to look more "natural." In Utah, this adaptation was taken a step further with the extensive use of brick—a material not commonly associated with Modernist design. What all this meant for the Mansion District was that its new buildings would reflect many of the basic visual ideas of Modernism while incorporating greater ornament and a broader range of materials.

The first of these more stylized buildings, the Moreton & Company Building at 641 East, was, like the Tracy Insurance Building, small and relatively simple. But its façade was visually more complex and stylistically more contemporary—a wall of windows framed in aluminum, giving the building an open, airy feel. All this was very much in the style of European Modernism. But the east end of the façade was set off by a grouping of "bookmatched" green marble panels that gave the simple structure an air of sophistication and elegance. Eight years later, Fred Moreton would incorporate many of the same features in developing a slightly larger building for the Fireman's Fund American Insurance Companies next door, to the east.

Across the street, a different form of modernization was taking place. Unlike the Moreton Building, the South Temple Professional Building at 770 East opened in 1958 without the demolition of an existing building. Nor, as with the Callister Clinic, did it even involve an extensive remodel. Instead, its owner, Dr. Joseph Kesler, chose to place a Modernist façade on a simple Victorian house. The new façade extended the front of the building sixteen feet to the north, incorporated expansive windows, added projecting wooden "fins" and flattened the roof to emphasize the building's new Modernist lines. Kesler's choice to remodel only the façade was new to South Temple, but the "slipcover" was becoming an increasingly common technique for modernizing façades of historic commercial buildings. For Kesler, the slipcover gave the old home the appearance that he was aiming for: that of a modern office building.

Moreton & Company was one of several insurance companies that pushed the migration of professional offices—and Modernism—farther east in the Mansion District. *Moreton & Company*.

Modernism was now the going trend in the Mansion District. Only two years after Moreton & Company completed its building, the Metropolitan Life Insurance Company moved into its new offices just to the west at 633 East. Compared to the Moreton Building, however, the Metropolitan Life Building represented something of a step back stylistically. In appearance, it was more like the Tracy Insurance Building—one story, brick, with little ornament. Like the Moreton Building, however, the Metropolitan Life Building incorporated natural materials as an ornamental element; on its southwest corner stood a column of native stone.

But the Metropolitan Life Building was not as significant for its architecture as it was for its ownership structure. It introduced a new approach to development in the Mansion District. To this point, properties in the Mansion District had been developed by local companies, with buildings typically named after the developer (e.g., Intermountain Clinic, Doxey-Layton Medical Center and Callister Clinic). The Metropolitan Life Building, however, was developed for and named after a national company, but it was built and owned by Salt Lake–based Majestic Investment, which leased it to Metropolitan Life. The principal and owner of Majestic Investment, Keith

Knight, would in 1962 follow the same ownership-leasing arrangement with AMCO-Utah Inc. for the IBM Building at 348 East.

As Modernism evolved in the Mansion District, it became more stylized, as in the case of the Orthopedic and Fracture Clinic at 702 East. The partners—Paul Pemberton, Robert Lamb and Mark Green—hired the Minnesota firm of Ellerbe and Company, which had specialized in the design of medical buildings. While a clinic may have seemed to require only a simple function design, Ellerbe and Company was accustomed to designing medical buildings that incorporated a flair for the dramatic. Most notable among these was the Diagnostic Building at the Mayo Clinic in Rochester, Minnesota.

The Orthopedic and Fracture Clinic, opened in 1961, made its own dramatic statement. It incorporated some of the same façade elements seen in the Moreton Building: an entry of aluminum-framed windows set off by green marble panels. Unlike that of the Moreton Building, which was almost entirely glass, the front façade of the Orthopedic and Fracture Clinic, except for the entry, was clad in cast-stone panels. Aluminum window frames protruded from the panels, giving the building an almost space age character. Even more dramatic, however, was a row of decorative concrete trellises projecting at right angles from the South Temple façade. Matching

The concrete trellises and marble panels of the Orthopedic and Fracture Clinic displayed Modernism's more ornate character. *Amanda Moore.*

trellises on the building's west side were set parallel to the building, doubling both as ornament and sun shades.

While the Orthopedic and Fracture Clinic presented new architectural ideas to the Mansion District, it followed what was by now a familiar pattern: the demolition of houses—in some cases, mansions—to make way for a new building and, of course, parking. All told, four structures were razed for the clinic, most notably the home associated with mining magnate Duncan MacVichie. Designed by Frederic Hale, one of Utah's most prominent architects, and completed in 1899, it had faced South Temple with an expansive porch, a striking dormer with three arched windows and—in appropriately grandiose Victorian style—a turret in its northwest corner.

The Orthopedic and Fracture Clinic brought to the Mansion District Modernism's more expressive persona. That expressiveness, however, would pale in comparison with the attitude of the Western General Agency Building, which demonstrated the extremes to which Modernism's austere aesthetic could be stretched. In 1964, Edward Mabey, a Salt Lake insurance broker and financier, purchased the modest Tracy Insurance Building. Based on what he did with it, it appears that Mabey had grand designs for the identity of his company. His modifications to the Tracy Insurance Building would represent a form of "branding" long before the term became fashionable in the world of marketing.

Over the next five years, Mabey completed a number of modifications that would completely alter the character of the building. First, he added a "thick flat roof"[126] to enhance the building's visual weight, sprayed the exterior with stucco into which were scribed arches that extended from the ground to the roof and installed expansive windows along the South Temple façade that allowed passersby to view a conference room with a circular colonnade of arches carried through from the exterior. Perceptive observers might even have been able to see the glass chandelier imported from Czechoslovakia hanging in the conference room.

Only four years later, Mabey remodeled the building again, adding an extravagant second-floor apartment for entertaining, replete with Corinthian columns in the hall, twenty-four-karat gold fixtures in the bathroom and hand-painted murals throughout. The exterior now sported lofty arches that extended two stories over the windows on the north (South Temple) and east sides. Windows ran along a second-story balcony, which was highlighted by decorative railings. Eventually, Mabey would even add a pool on the south side of the second floor.

The Western General Agency Building represented Modernism's most exuberant persona. It did not, however, represent a trend in the Mansion

Edward Mabey undertook a series of elaborate modifications to the Tracy Insurance Building that produced South Temple's most dramatic example of New Formalism. *Utah Heritage Foundation.*

District. The next generation of new buildings would bring back the more reserved principles of Modernism that focused on basic forms and contrasting materials rather than on applied ornamentation. Such was the building envisioned by Richard Steiner and his architect, Bill Browning, for the property occupied by the Weir-Cosgriff mansion at 505 East.

Steiner was the president of the Steiner American Corporation, an industrial linen supply company, and sought to construct a new building to house Steiner American's administrative functions. It's likely that the choice of location on South Temple was attributable, at least in part, to a sense of nostalgia on Steiner's part. His obituary in 2005 described how, as a child, "he would sometimes ride from the Fort Douglas stable down South Temple to see his grandparents."[127]

Browning was one of the principals in the Utah architectural firm Scott Louie and Browning, whose most senior partner, Carl Scott, had designed the Masonic temple and the Intermountain Clinic Building just down the street from the Weir-Cosgriff mansion. Along with the Steiner American Building, Browning would design some of Salt Lake's most significant Modernist structures, including the J.C. Penney Building at 310 South Main Street and the Wilde Wood Tower at 515 East 100 South.

In 1965, when the Steiner Foundation purchased the property at 505 East, it was still occupied by the mansion, "a formidable architectural statement in its own right."[128] Constructed in 1900 for Thomas Weir, it had been designed by one of Utah's most influential architects: Walter Ware. Built of yellow sandstone, it faced South Temple with "two flanking turrets and a roof deck [that] complemented the classically styled entry with its white Corinthian columns that stood out against the yellow sandstone of the grand structure." Inside, its fifteen rooms incorporated "conveniences considered luxury items of the day."[129]

Unlike the demolition of other Mansion District landmarks like the Chisholm home or the Dooly mansion, the demolition of the Weir-Cosgriff mansion in 1965 was a noteworthy event. "The razing of this sixty-five-year-old mansion," wrote historian Margaret Lester, "suddenly shocked the community into an awareness that the architectural legacy it assumed would be permanent was as unsteady as quicksand."[130] Browning himself was acutely aware of the ramifications of the demolition. "We knew the situation," he recalled. "We knew the public interest in tearing down Cosgriff." But community scrutiny didn't end with the demolition. "We knew exactly how it would be accepted," Browning said of the new building. "In fact, we worried a lot about it from the firm's standpoint—ourselves, our own reputation."[131]

It's important to note, however, that Richard Steiner did not purchase the property with the express intent of demolishing the mansion. In fact, his first step was to commission Scott Louie and Browning to undertake a study of how the mansion and carriage house might be reconfigured to accommodate the company's offices. Steiner's instructions to Browning's firm were to "take the existing [building] and see what you can do with it—understanding, of course, that the interior would be totally changed. We even investigated a connection—using the carriage house with a connection. But by the time that we did that, there was absolutely no parking on the entire site."[132]

So Browning's primary challenge was to design a new building that provided adequate office space as well as what was by now a requisite in the Mansion District: a parking lot. Even more daunting, however, was how to make a contemporary office building fit in with its neighbors. "Because of its location and the historical context of the street," Browning recalled, "scale was *really* important. It did not want to have a large scale. And therefore in my mind, it had to be broken up into more than just a box. A box of that square footage would have been totally obnoxious in that location and not compatible at all."[133] Browning's solution was a series of interconnected "boxes."

The Steiner American Building was acknowledged, even by those adamantly opposed to the demolition of the Weir-Cosgriff mansion, to be an architectural milestone in the Mansion District. *Amanda Moore.*

But scale wasn't the only issue of compatibility. *Salt Lake Tribune* columnist Robert Woody noted prior to the building's construction that "in materials and composition, it evokes—but does not imitate some of the design and structural materials of E. South Temple's mansion row." The primary material in question was brick, which reinforced the masonry heritage of Brigham Street and brought a more traditional palette to an otherwise contemporary building. Browning's Modernist touch? Running the courses of brick vertically instead of horizontally, creating a subtle perpendicular contrast to the building's horizontal profile. Browning complemented the brick with concrete columns that, according to Robert Woody, "suggest the columns of the neighboring structures."[134]

In communicating a distinctive Modernist identity while harmonizing with buildings several decades older, the Steiner American Building represented a watershed in South Temple's architectural history. To be sure, there was resentment within the community about the loss of the Weir-Cosgriff mansion. But that attitude was tempered by a growing recognition of the new building's significance. Perhaps most surprising was the assessment offered by Stephanie Churchill, first executive director of the Utah Heritage

Foundation. Churchill, who had been conspicuously vocal about what she perceived to be the unruly intrusion of Modernism on South Temple, was almost effusive about Browning's design: "The Cosgriff house was ripped down, but the anomaly to that is that it was ripped down for the Steiner American Building to be built. And it's probably the best new building on South Temple because of the way it fits into the context of the street. It's somewhat of a consolation that the Cosgriff home was replaced by a building of high quality."[135]

Even at its completion, there was a realization that the Steiner American Building was significant. One thousand people attended its opening reception in 1967, including Governor Calvin Rampton, who symbolically opened the building with "a snip of the towel."[136] The scene was reminiscent of the lavish social gatherings of a half century earlier. "Guests strolled through the grounds as if at a South Temple garden party," wrote historian Leonard Arrington.[137]

The construction of the Steiner American Building brought to a close an eventful period in the Mansion District. In a brief ten-year span, a number of the properties in the Mansion District had been "modernized," either through remodeling or new construction. As impactful as the architectural changes, however, were the changes in use. With the completion of the Steiner American Building, medical and professional office buildings (including historic buildings converted to office space) would occupy over 40 percent of the properties, whereas only forty years earlier these uses had been nonexistent in the properties between 500 East and 800 East. In only four decades, the Mansion District had transformed from an upscale residential area to a Modernist office park.

That transformation was facilitated by changes in zoning, particularly a Planning Commission amendment to the zoning ordinances in the mid-1950s that authorized "limited office" as an acceptable use in the Mansion District. (The Intermountain Clinic, Doxey-Layton Medical Center and Callister Clinic would have been considered "clinics," an already acceptable use.) The ostensible goal of the amendment was to encourage the adaptive reuse of the Mansion District's grand mansions, thereby ensuring their preservation.

But the Planning Commission, however well intentioned, was unconsciously following the law of unintended consequences. As architect Peter Emerson noted, the amendment prompted as much as it discouraged demolition and new construction. The impact on the Mansion District of the expansion of acceptable uses was amplified by a concurrent ordinance requiring off-street parking. Again, the goal, ostensibly, was to facilitate the reuse of existing homes—in this case, their conversion to apartments. Although a number of homes were converted—particularly farther east in the Upper East—the effect of the off-street requirement was to encourage further demolition. Far from being a regulatory burden, it represented a boon to some companies like Moreton, which touted the availability of its off-street parking in the grand opening ad for its new South Temple building. For others, like the Steiner American Corporation, it presented a conundrum. To comply with the parking ordinance, Steiner American would have to create additional parking space. Bill Browning's solution: locating the parking beneath the new building.

Although construction of new buildings abated with the completion of the Steiner American Building, the Mansion District continued to evolve. Perhaps the most significant event was the demolition in 1970 of the Dern mansion at 715 East by the Woodbury Corporation, a Salt Lake real estate firm. Woodbury had occupied the mansion for ten years but had apparently lost interest in its maintenance or use. So, in 1970, it was torn down to make way for nothing more than a vacant lot.

However, Woodbury's choice was the exception. Other mansions were successfully converted to offices housing small companies, including the Keith mansion at 539 East (for offices of Terracor, a land development company), the Joseph Richards mansion next door (for offices of the architectural firm of Brixen and Christopher) and the Daniel Jackling mansion across J Street from the Dern mansion (for offices of the law firm of Mitsunago and Ross). Ironically, and perhaps too late, these rare conversions demonstrated that the goal of the mid-1950s zoning amendment could be met.

Half a block to the east of the now-vacant Dern property sat another vacant lot. Unlike the Dern property, this one had been vacant for years—forty years, to be exact—since the Judge siblings had demolished the family mansion in 1933. Built in 1896 by Mary Judge, the mansion at 737 East was known as a social hub, "the scene," as described by the *Salt Lake Tribune*, "of some of the gayest parties of the gay nineties, a hospitable home filled with treasures."[138]

For nearly thirty years, the vacant property went through a series of owners, including the Intermountain Clinic Building Company, which considered constructing a parking lot on the site. It sat fallow until 1973, when it was purchased by Jean and Dick Westwood. Jean was well known in Utah political circles, having been active in Democratic politics at the state and national levels. Along with Jean's personal political aspirations, however, the Westwoods also had shared ambitions. They had recently retired as successful mink farmers and had, through the encouragement of Dick's brother, taken up the real estate development business.

In 1973, the Westwoods applied for and received a variance from the Salt Lake Board of Adjustment to construct an office building on the former site of the Judge mansion (as well as a vacant lot to the east). That fall, however, Dick fell off a ladder while picking apples, sustaining fractures to his neck and lower back that caused temporary paralysis. As a result, he became sensitive to cold temperatures, so he and Jean moved to Arizona, leaving behind the incipient project on South Temple.

Having abandoned their plans for an office building, the Westwoods sold their property to developer F.C. Stangl. Stangl had been active in the Salt Lake construction market, completing a diversity of buildings, including the Empire Building on 400 South, the IRS Building at the corner of 500 East and 400 South and the Canyon Apartments on Canyon Road. Like the Westwoods, Stangl was able to obtain a variance to construct an office building on the Judge property and hired architect Ron Molen, who produced a building that reflected the evolution of Modernist architectural thinking. With its deep-set windows, sense of regularity and modestly decorative brickwork, it struck a balance between the austerity of early Modernism and the later influences of ornamentation and natural materials.

The building was named for its tenant, Xerox, which assumed occupancy in 1974. But the building didn't belong to the company. It belonged to Stangl, who, much like Keith Knight had with Metropolitan Life, leased the building to Xerox. The arrangement represented a fitting close to the Mansion District's transformation. Properties that had once been occupied by wealthy Salt Lake families whose tenure seemed permanent were now being occupied by out-of-state corporations with only an ephemeral financial commitment.

The period of change in the Mansion District would, however, end on a very different note, one that presaged a new era for Brigham Street. It carried a tone of concern, of urgency, that South Temple's architectural heritage was disappearing. Nowhere was that sense of urgency more immediate than in the Mansion District. The change of pace in the Mansion District had accelerated since the mid-1950s (not coincidentally, the time when the zoning ordinance was amended to allow office buildings). Between 1925 and 1957, only three new buildings had been constructed in the Mansion District—one of those being the Masonic temple. But over the next seventeen years, nearly 25 percent of the properties in the Mansion District had been altered in some way. And six of those changes had involved the demolition of significant historic homes or mansions, including the

MacVichie, Weir-Cosgriff and Dern mansions. Not surprisingly, Salt Lake residents had taken notice.

By the late 1960s, many Salt Lakers found themselves agreeing with Margaret Burton, who expressed an increasingly widely held perception that South Temple was on the path to devastation. "Mature vandalism masquerading as progress," she wrote, "wantonly demolishes cherished landmarks of aristocratic distinction and historic significance." Burton decried the "construction of unattractive geometric monstrosities" and noted that "to date no feasible method has been formulated for reasonable control of the out-of-hand modernity."[139]

Anxiety continued to intensify. In 1974, the *Deseret News* summarized the increasing tension associated with Modernism's appearance along Brigham Street. "The new buildings that have surrounded and replaced our famous structures are often inhuman objects," wrote the *News*, paraphrasing Stephanie Churchill. According to Churchill, they reflected "a society in which machines do everything but give birth. They look as if they could have been designed by a computer."[140]

By the early 1970s, the concern for South Temple's past and future—prompted by the changes in the Mansion District—had transformed into an agenda: to establish a historic district that would provide protections for the street's historic properties. That agenda was carried to the City and County Building, and in 1975, the Salt Lake City Planning Commission approved an ordinance "designed to preserve old mansions and regulate new architecture on South Temple street."[141] The proposed ordinance gave the city power to prohibit demolition of historic buildings and deny the proposed design for a new building.

Unfortunately, the new rules did not some soon enough for two mansions built by two brothers—Alexander and Louis Cohn—just east of the Masonic temple. "The homes are not significant—except they are old," argued F. Gerald Irvine, president of the Masonic temple Association, as the Masons prepared to demolish them. "We feel a garden would look better east of our large Temple than these old rundown houses do."[142]

The demolition of the two grand mansions represented the draconian changes that had spurred the establishment of the South Temple Historic District. But demolition was only a symptom of change. The Mansion District had, between 1925 and 1975, transformed into a very different place, a busy corporate and medical hub. That transformation was the result not of demolition, per se, but of changes in ownership that, in turn, initiated changes in use. Quite simply, the lifestyle of Brigham Street had not been sustainable.

THE UPPER EAST

South Temple's Neighborhood

The Cottage was an unpretentious home at 1108 East South Temple built in 1907 by Patrick J. Moran for his mother-in-law. She died before it was completed, but Patrick and his spouse, Dolly, decided to move from their much larger, more elegant home on the corner to live in the Cottage. The downsizing may have been prompted by the fact that Moran, who was in the construction business (his projects included, most notably, paving of much of the street and sidewalks of South Temple), was experiencing intensifying financial difficulties. So, in 1932, Prudential Insurance, which held a mortgage on Moran's property, foreclosed. Four years later, the Cottage was purchased by W. Harold Dalgleish, a professor of history at the University of Utah.

Other than the unfortunate circumstances behind it (whether related or not, Moran died the same year), the transaction was not, in and of itself, a remarkable event. What was remarkable was that members of the Dalgleish family proceeded to live at 1108 East for the next seventy years. Remarkable, that is, when considering the turnover along most of South Temple but not so remarkable, as it turns out, for the "Upper East," the easternmost section of South Temple from 800 East to 1300 East. Unlike the rest of South Temple, the Upper East passed through the period between 1925 and 1975 with relatively little change. Its story is that of a place that, early on, established a distinct identity—and retained it.

The Dalgleishes were not unique. They moved in. And they stayed. Although their tenure was longer than most, the evolution of the Upper East

Patrick Moran's "Cottage" was the home of the Dalgleish family for seventy years. *Utah Heritage Foundation.*

was grounded, almost literally, in stories like theirs. From its earliest years, the Upper East was almost exclusively residential. And it stayed residential because its residents *stayed*.

The key to the stability of a place is, well, stability. The less turnover in ownership and/or use, the more likely that a place will retain its character. Houses in the Upper East just didn't turn over. So it was that in 1942, William and Dora Gallenson moved into their home at 926 East, on the corner of Haxton Place and South Temple, and lived there the rest of their lives. Only after Dora's death in 1984 did their son, Marvin, sell the property. In 1921, Walter and Marguerite Pugh purchased the home at 1224 East, where they raised their two children and which they and their family owned for fifty-two years. In 1904, John and Jennie Lynch moved into a home at 1167 East that they had purchased directly from its builder, William Hatfield. Their family retained ownership for a full fifty-five years.

These examples aren't meant to suggest that there wasn't turnover. There was—but not nearly to the degree found along the rest of the street. Even if properties changed ownership, with only few exceptions they stayed in the same use—as single-family residences. This was inherently a residential neighborhood, and its occupants would make sure that it stayed that way.

This photo, taken at 1100 East in the early 1900s, shows the beginnings of the quiet residential neighborhood that was and still is the Upper East. *Utah State Historical Society.*

This continuity of ownership extended to larger properties in the district that might have been attractive for nonresidential types of development. Surprisingly, the largest single properties along the entire length of South Temple (with the exception of Temple Square) lay not where they might have been expected—say, in the West End or even in the Church Blocks—but in the Upper East: the north half of the block between 1000 East and 1100 East, belonging to the Sisters of the Holy Cross, and combined lots on the north and south sides of South Temple between 1100 East and 1200 East, belonging to the Salt Lake Board of Education. Between 1925 and 1975, those properties did not change ownership.

But attributing the Upper East's stability to a minimum of turnover is somewhat simplistic. There were other factors at play. Zoning, in particular, defined how this district would evolve. The earliest zoning ordinances designated the five blocks as "Residential B," a classification that allowed only homes, apartments and "hotels" (essentially a synonym for apartments).

Functionally, that designation did not change. While the zoning of the Lower East opened the door for a whole smorgasbord of uses and that of the Mansion District facilitated its transformation into an office park, the zoning of the Upper East kept it just the way it was in 1925.

The influence of the Upper East's zoning designation was significantly strengthened by the lack of what might be termed "pre-existing conditions." In 1925, over 80 percent of all the properties in the district were occupied by single-family homes. There was no bakery. No grocery store. No pharmacy. No one commuted to offices in the Upper East. Or did any banking. Or visited their attorney. The only commercial presence in 1925 was that of service stations on the east and west corners of M Street and South Temple. So as Salt Lake City began designating zoning districts in the late 1920s, there were no precedents, no "noses in the tent" that could set a baseline for diversification. Over the next fifty years or so, the Upper East would be the only area of South Temple in which sustained commercial activity would not appear—at all.

However, the absence of any commercial activity in the Upper East could just as well be attributed to geography as to zoning. In 1925, the Upper East was removed from Salt Lake's business center downtown. As a result, it was insulated. A commercial business would naturally have desired a location closer to downtown. And though the University of Utah lay just to the east, its real period of growth and influence wouldn't occur until after World War II. In the middle of the twentieth century, there just wouldn't have been a reason to build a store or office building or medical clinic way up at the east end of South Temple.

This quality of being removed would have enhanced the Upper East's appeal as a residential neighborhood. And compared with South Temple's other residential neighborhood—the Mansion District—the Upper East would have had a much broader market, ensuring that as properties did turn over they would remain residential. The reason? They were simply much more affordable. Consider, for example, that in 1926 a group of Jewish investors purchased the Wall mansion at 411 East at the heavily discounted (about 80 percent) price of $100,000, while only a decade earlier, Paul Keyser had purchased the Louis Terry home at 1229 East, described by the *Salt Lake Tribune* as "one of the show places of Salt Lake," for only $40,000.[143] To be sure, the Wall mansion was much larger and the grounds much more expansive. Nevertheless, the opportunity to purchase "one of the show places" of the community (that, by the way, contained thirteen rooms and "commodious quarters for servants") on its most prestigious street for less

The Terry residence was typical of those in the Upper East—large and comfortable but smaller and less elaborate than those just to the west in the Mansion District. *Utah State Historical Society*.

than half the price of a grand mansion would have attracted a significantly greater number of prospective buyers.

Other houses in the Upper East, although smaller than the Terry home, were still relatively large and elaborate. But they would also have been in reach of many more Salt Lakers than would the estates just to the west. And some carried the appeal of a distinguished provenance. Architects of residences in the Upper East were among Utah's most distinguished, including Richard Kletting, Frederick Hale and Ware and Treganza.

The Upper East's residents were not, like those who had settled in the Mansion District, the fabulously rich. But they were wealthy. And they were influential. They included leaders in business, government and religion. Residents of the Upper East frequented the Alta Club and the University Club. They belonged to country clubs. Their parties appeared in the social pages of the local papers. The stability that informed the Upper East therefore derived not only from the fact that it was almost immutably residential in character. It derived, as well, from its residents—people with money and leverage who could wield the political influence to manage how the Upper East evolved.

So fundamentally residential was the Upper East that it may have seemed to be exclusively a neighborhood of single-family homes. But it did incorporate other uses. The most common of these was, quite naturally, apartments, which were simply a different form of living space. Or perhaps not so simply, if the first apartment building constructed after 1925 was any indication. It was to be, according to the headline in the *Salt Lake Tribune* in March of 1927, a "Big Apartment House," a prospect that prompted several neighbors to protest its construction in a "stormy hearing" before the City Commission that same month.[144] However, the City Commission ultimately overrode the protests and granted Bowers Building Company permission to construct the controversial structure.

With the somewhat incongruous name of the Mayflower, it would live up to its "Big" billing, standing five stories tall and stretching 127 feet along South Temple and over 200 feet along U Street. (Until the construction of Moreau Hall over twenty years later, the Mayflower would stand as the largest building in the Upper East.) Its grand scale was matched by its elaborate style. Designed by Slack Winburn (whose diverse credits would range from modest post–World War II homes in Rose Park to the towering First Security Building at 400 South Main), it reflected in contrast to its name "a modification of the Italian style"[145] or what an architectural historian would later term "Italian Renaissance."[146]

As elaborate as its exterior might have been, it paled in comparison to the apartments inside. A 1939 sales ad by Tracy Loan and Trust referred to them as "palatial." There were twenty in all, each with eight rooms, including three bedrooms, three bathrooms and maids' quarters. (Just in case, the basement held rooms for "extra maids and extra chauffeurs.") At the Mayflower's opening in 1928, an ad promoting investment in the property declared that it "contains all of the conveniences of the most modern home."[147] Other articles at the time also referred to the apartments not as apartments but as "homes." Bowers Building also went to great lengths to emphasize that the Mayflower was fireproof—a "modern" feature, especially considering that most of the apartment buildings in Salt Lake were not. (The same year that the Mayflower opened, two children were killed in a fire at the Normandy Apartments, prompting a review of city fire ordinances.)

Although the Mayflower would be called "one of the city's 'elite'" residential buildings,[148] twilight was setting in on the glamour years of apartment living. Luxury was no longer the byword. Convenience would become the rule. Apartments focused on offering modern amenities rather than on luxurious features. The styling of apartment buildings became less ornate, reflecting, as well, the sparer Modernist design influences that were beginning to appear in the United States.

Such was the case with the Commodore Apartments at 1107 East. Completed two years later, it was only slightly smaller than the Mayflower (four instead of five stories) but significantly more reserved in appearance. The Commodore was something of an architectural hybrid. Its lines anticipated the rectilinear forms of Modernism, particularly the flat roof highlighting its projecting wings and the picture windows reinforcing its horizontality. Its ornamentation was understated—just narrow bands of contrasting brick laid vertically—probably an economic choice. But its multicolored brick was a throwback to Period Revival styles, as was its grand entrance with a lofty arch and tall, multi-paned casement windows. These more decorative elements were tucked back—hidden almost—between the wings, as if to downplay their visual impact. (In the early 1960s, the entrance was remodeled to a more contemporary aesthetic.)

While the Commodore may have lacked the luxury or ornamentation of the Mayflower, it was, as one ad claimed, "ultra-modern" in its relative plethora of conveniences. Not only did it offer electric refrigerators, but it also offered electric ranges and gas water heaters. Its tenants had the exclusive use of what by that time would have been considered not a convenience but a necessity: a private garage.

The construction of the Mayflower and Commodore within two years of each other might have foreshadowed an apartment building land rush in the Upper East. But it's important to note that the Mayflower took up two lots, the larger of which had been vacant, while the entire lot on which the Commodore was constructed had been vacant. These buildings were, in many ways, opportunistic. They simply filled space that would otherwise have sat empty.

Constructing other apartment buildings of the size of either the Mayflower or the Commodore in the Upper East would have been significantly more complex, because there just weren't any privately owned properties of sufficient size. Building another apartment as large as either the Commodore or the Mayflower would have necessitated purchasing and consolidating several smaller properties. Negotiating with multiple owners would have entailed a process both complicated and (more problematic) time-consuming. And there would have been competition from other buyers—namely prospective homeowners—that would not have existed in other areas along South Temple. By 1930, it simply would have been easier to build an apartment house somewhere else in the city (in the Lower East, for example, where vacant lots were common). So, it comes as no surprise that, over the next forty-five years, the Upper East saw the construction of only five new apartment buildings, two of which sat on the same lot.

The next one would not appear until after World War II. By this time, apartment house design was trending toward an even simpler, less ornate design than found in the Commodore. So simple, in fact, that this new apartment building didn't even have a name. Constructed in 1947 at 1007 East, it contained twelve apartments. While it incorporated subtle decorative elements, it was essentially a plain, two-story brick building. Its most notable feature was likely its builder, Dorothy Jensen, known as "Salt Lake City's first woman contractor,"[149] who had carved out a niche as the builder of what she marketed as "Personality Homes." Of her style, the *Salt Lake Tribune* noted, "Dorothy is not an extreme modernist of the Frank Lloyd Wright variety."[150] Her apartment building at 1007 East clearly demonstrated the point.

If Dorothy Jensen's design trended toward the plain and simple, then the construction in 1951 of the J. Hill Apartments at 848 East seemed to define an endpoint for that progression. The building was small—only a dozen one- and two-bedroom apartments—but it was its unadorned style that may have been its most (or least) prominent feature. Designed by its builder John Hill Johnson, the structure was notable for its lack of ornamentation—of any kind.

In its absence of style, it was simply a larger version of the tract homes being constructed following World War II. The desire of developers to build homes cheaply and quickly—coupled with a lack of resources due to the war—had generated a new approach using a limited inventory of materials. That simplified approach (and resulting spare style) extended to apartment buildings, and J. Hill Apartments was representative of so many small apartment buildings of that era. By 1950, the essence of apartment living had been distilled into one aspect: convenience. J. Hill Apartments was not marketed as luxurious in any sense of the word. The apartments' most notable features? Electric ranges, electric refrigerators, electric fans, automatic garbage disposal units, garages and a laundry in the basement.

At this point, it may have seemed that apartment buildings in the Upper East needed a lift. And they would get it—stylistically and structurally—with the construction of the Bonneville Tower in 1965. Bonneville Tower lived up to its name, soaring a full fifteen stories over the South Temple landscape.

One would have to have ventured seven blocks to the west to the University Club Building to find a building close to that size on South Temple.

Bonneville Tower was only one of a plethora of high-rise apartment buildings being constructed in Salt Lake during the early 1960s. Rapid population growth had prompted a spike in the demand for housing, but the supply was woefully inadequate. In response, in 1963, the Utah legislature passed the Condominium Ownership Act, which effectively incentivized construction of new apartments and condos. By the time Bonneville Tower was on the drawing board in 1964, "Multi-Unit Construction [was] Moving at Speedy Pace." Apartment and condominium towers were sprouting like wildflowers around the city, prompting the *Salt Lake Tribune* to strike a cautionary tone. Quoting a report by the Utah Bureau of Economic and Business Review, the *Tribune* noted that "the general housing market is satiated."[151]

That assessment, as it turned out for the developers of Bonneville Tower, was gloomily prophetic. Nearly 2,700 units were authorized in 1963 alone, ten times the number that had been constructed only fifteen years earlier. By 1964, apartments in Salt Lake City were being constructed at three times the rate of the country as a whole. Nevertheless, Bonneville Tower's developer, Artcol Corporation, proceeded full speed ahead with construction, even as it was completing Sunset Tower just around the corner on 900 East and proposing a third building, Plaza Tower, for the corner of South Temple and A Streets. Between the two projects under construction, it had committed well over $6 million (over $46 million in 2015 dollars), all of which had been insured by the Federal Housing Administration. (The mortgage on Bonneville Tower was, up to that time, the largest processed by the FHA in Utah.)

Bonneville Tower was as grand as its investment. Its fifteen stories held over 240,000 square feet of living, parking and lounging space. Designed by Salt Lake architects Pat Harris and Harold Carlson, it didn't rely simply on its scale to project its grandeur. It was an elaborate expression of New Formalist ideas, an expressive blend of Modernist austerity and Classical ornament. Its Modernist shape—a rectangle stretching skyward—was juxtaposed by decorative elements: a grand arch over the main entrance, perforated concrete block screening the ground-floor parking garage and scrolled railings along the balconies. As it faced South Temple, the building stepped back at its third and tenth stories in an attempt to diminish its visual impact on the street.

With all its grandeur, however, what Bonneville Tower lacked was a sense of scale. Standing as tall as it did, it dwarfed every building around it and stood in marked contrast even with the huge mansions just to the west. Yet its

Bonneville Tower was the only high-rise residential building to appear on South Temple until the construction of condominiums at 99 West in 2010. *Amanda Moore*.

developers practically wallowed in its excess, claiming that it was "the most luxurious west of Chicago."[152] A 1966 ad for the building invited prospective residents to experience "elegance…luxury…carefree living."[153]

Not so carefree, as it turns out. By December 1966, less than a year after Bonneville Tower opened, Artcol was experiencing "financial difficulties."[154] The decline in demand for apartments projected by the *Salt Lake Tribune* only two years earlier had come to pass. As it turned out, Bonneville Tower was the "third major apartment in the Salt Lake Area this year that has run onto financial skids."[155] Unlike the 1940s and 1950s, when people were moving *to* Salt Lake City for jobs in energy or aerospace, now people were moving *away* from Salt Lake City, to the county's rapidly growing suburbs. An increase in apartment units combined with a decrease in population created an instant glut in the apartment market.

A year and a half after the opening of Bonneville Tower, only 32 of the 116 units had been sold. In December 1966, the FHA foreclosed. In a note of ironic hindsight, the *Salt Lake Tribune* explained that "overbuilding of apartments—particularly those with luxury rental units—has been blamed."[156] The building then proceeded to cycle through a series of owners, finally landing in the hands of Thompson Michie Associates, which purchased it in 1973 for less than the original construction cost.

Perhaps Artcol's excesses and subsequent tribulations influenced other developers, but Bonneville Tower would, until construction of 99 West almost fifty years later, be the only high-rise apartment to loom over South Temple. So it was natural that the last of the Upper East's apartment buildings would represent a return to a smaller, simpler form. In the late 1960s, B. Robert Clark and Partners constructed not one but two apartment buildings at 1259 East, one on the north side of the lot in 1965 and another on the east side four years later. Like the Majestic Apartments a few blocks away, they reflected the simple, unadorned style that had come to define small apartment buildings of the era.

But the unique aspect of Clark and Partners' development was that it kept the existing Viggo Madsen home, converting it to apartments. Its Revivalist detailing—quoins at the corners, heavy stone lintels and massive wooden door—stood in stark contrast to the minimalist buildings that now shared the property. It was a curious complex marketed with an even more curious name: Somerset Gardens. Clark and Partners evidently banked on the character of the Madsen home. Advertisements at Somerset Gardens' opening characterized it as "elegant" and "distinctive," terms that were, at the least, incongruous with the two new buildings.

While Clark and Partners' variation on it may have been original, the conversion of homes to apartments was, by the 1960s, a common occurrence in the Upper East. Between 1925 and 1960, over 25 percent of the homes in the Upper East would, at one time or another, be transformed to apartments. What's remarkable, however, is that, rather than diminishing the inherent residential character of the Upper East, all those conversions served only to reinforce it. The reason? Even as the interiors of the various homes were being carved up into apartments, their exteriors—with rare exception—were left essentially untouched.

Case in point, the Downey mansion. In 1893, Frederick Albert Hale designed an elaborate Shingle-style home for retired army major George Downey and his spouse, Lizzie, on the southeast corner of 800 East and South Temple. Dormers projected from the conical roof of a turret on the home's northwest corner. The expansive façade presented a grand porch and entry. Large gables on the north and west sides framed broad arches. Windows abounded—of all shapes and sizes. As if all these elements weren't enough, Hale added a note of contrast with the first story clad in stone and the upper two stories in shingles.

In 1937, Miles Miller, a Salt Lake architect, purchased the home and divided it into four apartments that he advertised as "modern," offering electric kitchens, hot water heaters and "beautiful outside grounds."[157] Over the years—and through a series of different owners—three more apartments were added, but the exterior of the Downey mansion retained its essential character. To the passerby, it would have looked much like the home that it was when it was built.

The Downey mansion exemplified the Upper East's salient quality. Even as it was changing, it was staying essentially the same. By all appearances, it remained a single-family residential neighborhood. With rare exception, the conversions of homes to apartments were accomplished without changing their external appearance. They still *looked* like homes. Even when Clyde Harvey purchased the Downey mansion in 1974 and converted the former apartment house to offices, he retained its original appearance. (Harvey actually undertook an extensive restoration of the entire building.)

As the Downey mansion demonstrated, the houses of the Upper East were suitable for a variety of uses—not just as homes. As with homes, however, these other uses were "low-density"—they didn't generate a lot of activity. As a result, they could be readily accommodated by the existing structures. They included other forms of residential use, in particular nursing and "rest homes" that proliferated in the 1950s and 1960s. Nonresidential uses

Typical of apartment conversions in the Upper East, the Downey mansion was occupied by apartments (here, the Gloria Apartments in 1949) for over thirty years yet retained its essential exterior appearance. *Utah State Historical Society.*

included clubs, social/charitable organizations and small medical clinics. All of these fit quite nicely into existing homes, as exemplified by the Town Club, which moved into the Frances Walker home at 1081 East in 1940. The presence of various clubs would have had an almost imperceptible impact on the residential character of the Upper East.

That's not to say that architectural change was, with the exception of the few new apartment buildings, absent from the Upper East. In 1949, acknowledging that the need for a training facility for nurses was "urgent," Holy Cross Hospital launched a fundraising drive to raise half of the $1 million needed to construct the building at the corner of 1000 East and South Temple.[158] In September of that year, the cornerstone was laid for what would become the Holy Cross School of Nursing, and a year later, the new school was dedicated. The ceremony was significant enough to warrant attendance by Utah governor J. Bracken Lee and Salt Lake mayor Earl Glade, as well as by Mother Rose Elizabeth, mother superior of the Order of the Holy Cross.

This building constructed for the Ladies Literary Club in 1912 fit quite comfortably into the residential fabric of the Upper East. *Author's collection.*

Designed by Lloyd McClenahan, the Holy Cross School of Nursing (named Moreau Hall after Basil Moreau, founder of the Order of Holy Cross) was, for the Upper East, an imposing building. Although its five-story profile was essentially horizontal, its lines asked the observer to gaze up rather than along the building. Tall windows were arranged in columns framed by brick pilasters highlighted at the top with concrete caps that informed the pilasters with an upward momentum. But the building's most dramatic vertical element was its entrance. Angled toward the corner of South Temple and 1000 East, its entry door was set off by a shallow arch. The upper stories of the entry façade were clad in fluted concrete panels whose vertical lines carried through rows of windows ending in delicate tips that pointed to an alcove containing a large cross.

The nursing school operated in Moreau Hall until 1973, when it graduated its last class with "the traditional procession down South Temple from the school at 1002 E. South Temple to the Cathedral of the Madeleine."[159] The building was then closed temporarily before reopening as the Holy Cross Family Health Center. It also housed the Family Practice Residency program from the University of Utah College of Medicine and the Therapeutic Living Center, "an 'early intervention' partial hospitalization program for alcoholics and others with psychiatric problems."[160]

Moreau Hall occupied the northwest corner of a block that was owned entirely by the Sisters of the Holy Cross. The south half was dominated by the ever-enlarging Holy Cross Hospital built in 1904. But the northeast quarter of the block had sat vacant since the city was settled. So forlorn was this corner that the *Deseret News* remarked that it had once been "an alfalfa field occupied by a lone horse."[161]

In 1939, the horse and alfalfa would give way to what the *Salt Lake Tribune* would glowingly term a "sea of beauty."[162] That year, the Utah Rose Society opened its municipal rose garden. The garden contained more than one hundred varieties of roses and more than six thousand plants, many of which were donated by an unlikely assortment of organizations, including the Utah Federation of Music Clubs, the Salt Lake Auxiliary of the Utah Woolgrowers Association and the Sagebrush Democrats. At its peak, the garden, covering five acres, was one of the largest in the United States. In 1972, however, it was quite literally uprooted to make way for the most antithetical use conceivable: a parking lot.

While the rose garden played a special role in the life of the hospital and of the broader community, it played perhaps an even more important role in the development of the Upper East. It was, after all, a garden. As such, it reinforced the Upper East's ambiance as a quiet residential neighborhood. That quality was even further reinforced by the fact that only a handful of nonresidential buildings would be constructed east of 800 East between 1925 and 1975. And following the completion of Moreau Hall in 1950, only two smaller ones would appear in the next twenty-five years.

The first, the Stevenson Clinic at 935 East, was modest in size but expansive in its interpretation of Modernist architectural ideas. The Stevensons were a family of doctors who were sharing a cramped space in the Medical Arts Building when they decided in 1959 to move to South Temple and commissioned Utah architect Burtch Beall to design a new building for their diverse practices. As Beall recalled, the Stevensons sought a "contemporary look" for the clinic. His design utilized trendy materials, most notably a paneled "window-wall" system—metal-framed windows set off by tan panels above and below—that covered the rest of the building. "Paneled systems," noted Beall, "were becoming all the rage."[163]

With its rectilinear lines and modern materials, the clinic contrasted with the older homes of the Upper East. Its design (particularly the large

With its panelized wall system, the Stevenson Clinic brought to the Upper East in 1959 the latest trend in Modernist design. *Burtch Beall.*

stone panel) represented the kinder, gentler persona of Modernism that had emerged in Utah in the 1950s and 1960s, as divergent ideas migrated from the Bay Area, where architects were softening European Modernism's hard edges with natural materials. Beall adapted these ideas by incorporating a two-story column of natural stone on the clinic's South Temple façade.

The Upper East's foray into Modernism would take a final step with the construction in 1974 of the AFCO Building at 807 East. Like the Stevenson Clinic, the new building was rectilinear—all straight lines and right angles. Two-story brick columns framed large recessed windows, while the building's third story featured a row of smaller windows set off by white concrete. The AFCO Building was an abrupt change from the grand Victorian mansion that had occupied the property for seventy-five years. Built for furniture dealer Henry Dinwoodey in 1890, the mansion had been designed by Richard Kletting, architect of the Utah State Capitol.

Yet the AFCO and the other few Modernist buildings that appeared east of 800 East between 1925 and 1975 had little impact on the Upper East's inherently residential character. What *was* changing was the nature of that character. By the mid-1960s, apartments passed single-family homes as the primary use in the Upper East. Together, apartments and homes constituted over 60 percent of all uses. However, conversions represented about 80 percent of apartments. So even as the types of residences were changing, the Upper East remained a residential neighborhood with a distinctly residential character.

"THE RICHNESS OF HUMAN VARIATION"

In a study published in 1975 (the same year that the South Temple Historic District was created), a group of University of Utah law students remarked that "little has been done in the past 50 years to improve or maintain South Temple's character."[164] It may have been unappreciative of the new buildings that had appeared during that period, but their perspective reflected the thinking of much of the community at the time. For many, South Temple—particularly the eastern section known as Brigham Street—had suffered from what might, at a minimum, be termed a decline, and the new buildings that had appeared between 1925 and 1975 were at best incompatible with Brigham Street's grand mansions and at worst downright ugly. Especially galling was that in some cases they replaced buildings of tremendous architectural beauty and historical significance.

The creation in 1975 of the South Temple Historic District represented an attempt to stem the perceived decline and preserve and perhaps even restore east South Temple Street's earlier grandeur. As the *Deseret News* had suggested a few years earlier, "If there had been an Historical Advisory Council in the past, the community might have avoided such mistakes as the demolition of the old Salt Lake Theater or the historic Cosgriff home on South Temple."[165] Like all historic districts, South Temple's was intended to at least slowly change. According to the *Deseret News*, the protections afforded by the creation of the district would "help prevent the community's historical heritage from being chewed up by bulldozers or allowed to rot away."[166]

The simple matter, however, was that, just as change on South Temple didn't suddenly commence in 1925, it didn't—and couldn't—suddenly end in 1975. More to the point, some of the most significant buildings along South Temple have appeared only in the last forty years. Yet even as the street inexorably evolves, the places of South Temple have retained their essential identities. The West End still sits isolated from the rest of the community—in spite of various grand ideas for "revitalizing" it. The Church Blocks continues to manifest two very different personae, even as its south side has gone through yet another complete makeover. The Lower East is still a jumble with even greater disparity in scale, style and use. The progression of the Mansion District to an office park has continued apace. And the Upper East remains very much the same place that it was nearly one hundred years ago.

THE WEST END: "A REAL SENSE OF ACTIVITY"

In 1991, Salt Lake welcomed a new arena: the Delta Center, named after its corporate sponsor, Delta Airlines. (The arena has since gone through two name changes.) A large glass cube, it would occupy the entire block across South Temple from the Devereaux House. Though it looked starkly different than its predecessor, the Salt Palace (which was essentially a large concrete drum), it was hailed with the same hearty optimism that had greeted the Salt Palace less than twenty-five years earlier. "Delta Center breathes new life into area," pronounced the *Deseret News*, quoting Salt Lake Redevelopment Agency director Alice Steiner, who asserted that "there's a real sense of activity."[167] Steiner's happy assessment may have stemmed, at least in part, from what for the West End would have constituted a veritable whirlwind of construction activity in the previous twelve years, with three massive projects—Symphony Hall, the Salt Palace "Expo Center" and a new Holiday Inn—dramatically changing the landscape.

By far the most significant of these was the completion of Symphony Hall in 1979. For many in the community, it was a facility whose time had come. This was certainly the case for the Utah Symphony, which had, for the past thirty years, presented its performances in the Tabernacle in Temple Square. But an arts facility had been on the planning board for some time and was even contemplated as part of the Salt Palace complex before cost considerations ruled it out. Located on the site of Simon Bamberger's Interurban Depot

The construction in 1991 of the Delta Center (now called the Vivint Smart Home Arena) seemed to herald a new era for the West End. *Author's collection.*

Building, Symphony Hall (which would later be renamed Abravanel Hall in honor of longtime Utah Symphony conductor Maurice Abravanel) was fêted at its grand opening with the ringing of church bells throughout the city.

Just next door to the west, the city's conference center would expand along South Temple four years later. Known, quite appropriately, as the "Salt Palace expansion," it would serve as exposition space to complement the meeting rooms in the main facility to the south. The expansion was accompanied by the construction of yet another conference hotel in the West End. Holiday Inn, which had failed twelve years earlier in a bid to construct a hotel on the site occupied by Howard Johnson, now built an even larger hotel a block to the west with "400 guest rooms, ballroom facilities for 800 persons, meeting rooms, a 'Holidome' recreation center, restaurant, lounge, and a physical connection to the new Salt Palace Exhibition Hall."[168] With all these new spaces for a diversity of activities—for the arts, for business, for sports and for lodging—Alice Steiner's optimistic appraisal would certainly seem to have been well founded. But even these massive projects couldn't diminish the West End's intransigent isolation.

Nevertheless, a sense of optimism endured. Ten years after the Delta Center hosted its first event, the Boyer Company opened the Gateway shopping center at the west end of the West End. The mall itself stretched south along 400 West, but the development absorbed the now abandoned Union Pacific Depot as event space. ("The grand old dame is tired," mourned the *Deseret News*.)[169] Even compared to Symphony Hall or the Exposition Center or the Delta Center, it was huge—500,000 square feet. Its tenants would include upscale retailers like Abercrombie & Fitch, J. Crew and Apple. It was to be "the centerpiece" for bringing vitality to the area neighboring the Union Pacific Depot known also as "the Gateway."[170]

Instead, the new shopping center found itself almost immediately contending with the West End's chronic isolation. Four years after Gateway's opening, the *Deseret News* noted that "some issues that challenged the ambitious project a year ago still remain. Retailers in the development say that weekday and Sunday traffic is still slower than they had hoped. And tenants still feel somewhat isolated from the rest of downtown."[171] Isolated they were. So much so that by 2015, less than fifteen years after its grand opening, Gateway was mired in what the *Salt Lake Tribune* characterized as a "deepening slump."[172]

But no development tells a more pointed story of the futility of trying to invigorate the West End than does the Triad Center. Its groundbreaking in June 1982 was eerily similiar to that of the Salt Palace and the Delta Center, with exuberant projections of its potential impact on the West End. "With the expansion of the Salt Palace on one end of the project and with Temple Square a block away on the other side," exclaimed Triad Utah president Emanuel A. Floor, "the Triad Center will be a boon to the area and revitalize historic South Temple Street to its original glory from the Union Pacific Depot to the Eagle Gate."[173]

Floor had good reason to be optimistic, if the scale of the concept were any indication. The plan for the two-and-a-half-block development called for two forty-story office buildings, three twenty-five-story condominiums and a hotel. Altogether, Triad America would construct nearly 2 million square feet of office space, over 1 million square feet of condominium space, 500,000 square feet of hotel and convention space and over 750,000 square feet of other uses. The list of proposed amenities was endless: a skating rink, a "European-style" farmers' market, an amphitheater, a "legitimate theater," athletic facilities, movie theaters, restaurants, a swimming pool, fountains, sculptures, even a "'yellow brick road' that will guide visitors through the center."[174] As if all that weren't enough, the overall concept incorporated

The demise of the grand plan for the Triad Center only underlined the reality of the West End's isolation. *EDA Architects.*

the Devereaux House. The Triad Center was nicknamed "The Gathering Place," a descriptive phrase ostensibly adopted from Brigham Young. So positive were the project's backers of its success that Triad America chairman Essam Khashoggi and his family "jetted into town" from Saudi Arabia for the groundbreaking's "day of dazzling pomp and pageantry."[175]

But the gathering didn't materialize. By 1984, only two smaller buildings had been constructed. More telling, however, Triad Center management had already become acutely aware of the project's isolation and had purchased three trolley buses in an attempt "to link Triad Center with downtown and local hotels."[176] Nevertheless, in June of the next year, Adnan Khashoggi traveled to Salt Lake for the groundbreaking of 1 Triad Center, a thirty-five-story office tower to be constructed just west of the Devereaux House. But the whole concept was already foundering, and in 1986, the Triad Center went into foreclosure. That same year, Adam & Smith sought a buyer for $5 million of structural steel that had been ordered for the new structure.

Certainly, the Triad Center's demise was due to a broader set of conditions than just its isolation. But a 1984 analysis of its design by architects Joseph Linton and Wayne Bingham made the pointed observation that "the Triad Center is a thread in the fabric of the city, but it does not link with other parts of the city....Those bridges which relate to other parts of the city do not exist at this point."[177]

Linton and Bingham's metaphor aptly described the gulf between the West End and the rest of the city. Those "bridges" to the West End were never built. Even today, the West End suffers from a lack of activity. It's dominated by massive structures that sit vacant more than they are utilized—Abravanel Hall, the Convention Center, Vivint Smart Home Arena, the Union Pacific Depot. Worse, much of the space in the West End has been lost to the most insidious of all uses: surface parking, vast expanses of asphalt that, too, are more often vacant than they are occupied.

The Church Blocks: Still "In Tune with the Times"

When LDS Church president David O. McKay in 1954 expressed the intent that ZCMI "keep in tune with the times," he set in motion a continual cycle of change in the Church Blocks. Prior to McKay's remarks, the south side of the Church Blocks had remained seemingly immutable. The most significant structures—the Templeton Building, the Deseret News Building, the Vermont Building and the Sharon Building—had all stood unaltered for over fifty years. Within twenty years following his remarks, however, all would be demolished or remodeled. But that period was almost calm compared with the next forty years, when the *entire* south side of South Temple between West Temple and State Streets underwent a complete metamorphosis. Actually, to be more accurate, the next thirty years. Today, not one building remains that stood before 1985. Gone are the Temple Square Hotel, the Beneficial Life Annex, the Deseret News Building, the Kennecott Building, the ZCMI Center, the Deseret Book Building, the Medical Arts Building and the Federal Reserve Bank—all of which were built or remodeled between 1925 and 1975 and some of which today would be considered architecturally and/or historically significant. Gone, too, is the massive Crossroads Mall, completed in 1985, with its "Richards Street" entrance opening on South Temple.

Beginning with the construction of the Eagle Gate Tower (*right*), the south side of the Church Blocks would once again undergo a complete transformation. *Author's collection.*

The essence of this remarkable transformation is reflected at the two ends of the Church Blocks. At the east end, on the site where the Federal Reserve Bank and Medical Arts Building once stood, rises the twenty-two-story Eagle Gate Tower. Completed in 1986, its design, according to LDS Church president Ezra Taft Benson, who presided over the ribbon cutting, was in keeping with the historic buildings across the street that were literally reflected in its mirrored glass.

Upscale condominiums replaced the Temple Square Hotel at the southeast corner of West Temple and South Temple in 2010. *Author's collection.*

At the west end of the Church Blocks stands 99 West, at thirty stories Salt Lake's tallest residential structure. Its construction in 2010 reflected the trend in urban planning to encourage more people to live downtown as a means of fostering more commercial activity there. Architecturally, it was something of a throwback—a "revival" perhaps—with curved corners derivative of the Moderne styles of the 1930s and 1940s.

Between these two towering bookends, most of the south side of the Church Blocks would in 2010 be taken over by the latest version of the grand downtown revitalization concept. "City Creek Center" elevated the concept of the enclosed shopping mall with an open pedestrian promenade, plazas and even a stream running through the middle. As with 99 West (which was itself part of the City Creek development), the buildings of City Creek Center were referential in their design, presenting contemporary interpretations of architectural ideas from the past. Nevertheless, even as the south side of the Church Blocks changed and changed again, the north side—Temple Square and Administrative Square—stayed resolutely the same.

The Lower East: Apartmentization's Next Wave—"Badly Needed Downtown Living Space"

Although it was incorporated in the South Temple Historic District, the Lower East by 1975 offered little to reinforce Brigham Street's historic character. Few of its buildings would have met the standards for being designated as "historic," and those were dispersed among structures of all sizes and styles. The fact was that there was no definitive character to the Lower East.

If the Lower East were to trend toward any particular identity over the next forty years or so, it would be toward that of an urban residential district. The "apartmentization" process that had briefly emerged in the 1920s reemerged at the end of the twentieth century, prompted by a perceived need to produce more "badly needed downtown living space."[178] By far, the most dramatic new entrant was the Brigham Apartments, completed in 1998. Containing over three hundred units and standing eight stories tall, it was larger than the Covey and Buckingham Apartments (just to the east) combined. In fact, it occupied by far the largest footprint of any building in the Lower East.

This second wave of apartmentization inflicted a significant casualty. Even the designation of the South Temple Historic District couldn't prevent the demolition of the Bransford Apartments on the corner of South Temple and Main Streets. Once considered the ultimate in luxurious urban living, it succumbed to "unexpected structural problems"[179] and was demolished in 1984 to make way for the Eagle Gate Apartments, a much less elaborate structure that incorporated "some architectural features"[180] of the Bransford Apartments.

Even today, the Lower East still grapples to achieve some architectural consistency. While the Brigham Apartments was ostensibly designed to fit

Completed in 1998, the massive Brigham Apartments signaled another wave of "apartmentization" in the Lower East. *Author's collection.*

into its context, simply by virtue of its size it exacerbates the Lower East's disparity of scale. Other buildings have brought even more stylistic diversity to the already eclectic mix. Primary among these is the building commonly referred to as "IBM II," constructed in 1981 at 402 East. Perhaps Salt Lake's prime example of "Brutalist" architecture, it presents a large, abstracted set of concrete forms capped by a band of ribbon windows. Just to the east sits the diminutive Backer's Bakery, as different a building from IBM II as could be imagined.

The story of the Lower East's uncertainty ultimately comes back to the earliest new building of the midcentury period. The Brown Motors/Crystal Palace/Makoff Building has, in its ninety-year lifetime, presented no fewer than four different façades to South Temple. The latest, a contemporary treatment of glass, aluminum and stone, has removed any trace of the "architectural innovation" designed by John Sugden for Samuel Makoff. Through its ever-changing persona, the Brown Motors/Crystal Palace/Makoff Building distills the tale of a place continually struggling to find an identity.

Epilogue

The Mansion District:
"Harmonize with the Traditional Style of the Street"

In 1925, the Mansion District was the epicenter of Brigham Street. Grand estates lined South Temple from 500 East to 800 East. This was a residential enclave that was beyond upscale. But within fifty years, all that had changed. Not a single property remained as a residence. And some didn't remain at all. The residential enclave had transformed into an office park.

Those mansions that did remain—Keith, Hogle, Kearns, Walker and others—now housed offices, social and charitable organizations (including an alcohol rehabilitation center) and even the governor of Utah (sometimes only ceremonially). Over time, these changes in function effectively extinguished the Mansion District's Brigham Street persona. They were accompanied by a continually changing set of architectural ideas that would alter Brigham Street's landscape.

No building, in fact, could have been architecturally more distant from the grand estates than the one constructed in the early 1980s between 500 and 600 East. Its construction demonstrated the fragility of the premise that the South Temple Historic District would preserve Brigham Street's remaining historic buildings. This new structure (or structures, depending on which development proposal was being discussed) would occupy the site of not one, but two significant historic buildings: the James Hogle mansion and the Second Church of Christ Scientist. And therein lay the rub. For the project lay inside the boundaries of what was then the pending historic district. The developers (which, somewhat ironically, included Hogle Investment) sought to have the boundary moved east to 600 East, thereby excluding the project from the restrictions that the district would have imposed. But their request was rendered moot when Salt Lake City relented and granted the requisite demolition permits.

Originally, the developers had proposed one large office. The concept then morphed into two smaller offices, ostensibly to fit in with the scale of the Mansion District (and, politically, to appease the preservation community). By the time construction on what was to be called Governor's Plaza actually began in the early 1980s, however, the concept had changed entirely from two smaller office structures to a complex with one six-story office building fronting South Temple Street and a twelve-story condominium building rising behind. "The office building is designed to step back and step down to the historic house to the east," wrote the

Governor's Plaza, the largest project in the Mansion District, demonstrated the fragility of the ordinances associated with the pending historic district. *Author's collection.*

architects, Edwards and Daniels. "The design provides the proper scale relationship with the street and neighbors."[181]

Whether Governor's Plaza was actually successful in achieving that goal, it's clear that the community conversation about the character of the historic district significantly influenced the thinking of its architects, who negotiated the design with the South Temple Historic Committee. That influence extended, as well, to two other buildings that appeared slightly earlier in the Mansion District.

The first of these, the U and I Building, was designed by one of Utah's most progressive architects, Dean Gustavson. Completed in 1976, it stood on the site occupied at one time by the Dern mansion that had been demolished in 1970 by the Woodbury Corporation. By the mid-1970s, U and I (short for Utah-Idaho Sugar Company) was looking for a new headquarters, because its current home, the Vermont Building at 51 West, was being demolished to make way for the Crossroads Mall.

As it contemplated construction of a new building on the now vacant lot, U and I confronted the limitations set by the pending ordinances associated with the establishment of the South Temple Historic District. Even though those ordinances (which would include review of new construction in the historic district) had yet to be passed, their presence affected Gustavson's approach to the building's design. "The client," Gustavson told the *Deseret News*, "is very concerned that the building meet esthetic [*sic*] objectives." To achieve that goal, "brick construction would be employed and the roof would not be a typical flat commercial building type."[182] Gustavson's concession? A mansard roof.

The result of this compromise was a rather curious architectural hybrid—a long, low Modernist structure with a mansard roof. Nevertheless, sounding very much like Edwards and Daniels, in its opening program, U and I asserted that "plans for the new building were carefully considered and drawn to provide a harmonious blend with the neighborhood.... The results, we feel, were very successful and add distinction to the neighborhood." U and I even went so far as to characterize its headquarters as "A New Landmark on South Temple in Salt Lake City."[183] What *wasn't* successful, apparently, was the location. Only four years later, U and I moved its headquarters to Pasco, Washington, and put the barely inhabited building up for sale for $3.8 million.

Gustavson's design set something of a standard for architects seeking to bring contemporary ideas to South Temple: brick construction with a mansard roof. For in 1978, the same combination of elements would appear on a late Modernist structure at 699 East South Temple. The Potomac Center, designed by Ron Molen, was conceived "to harmonize with traditional style of the street."[184] Like its mansion neighbors, the building was certainly visually complex, with extensive relief and varying window patterns, but it was clad in brick and topped with a mansard roof.

Fitting in visually with the historic buildings in the Mansion District was one thing. Fitting in functionally was another thing entirely. Whether these three new buildings—U and I, Potomac Center and Governor's Plaza—reinforced the historic character of the Mansion District is a matter of debate, but they most definitely did not reinforce the pattern of use from the era of Brigham Street. Along with conversion of the Mansion District's remaining historic homes, they added a punctuation mark to the progression of the three blocks between 500 East and 800 East from a quiet haven of extravagant estates to a bustling district of professional offices.

Epilogue

The Upper East:
Still South Temple's Neighborhood

On a stormy March day in 1986, a small group celebrated the groundbreaking for the new Ronald McDonald House by watching "Ronald McDonald and local dignitaries lift a clump of grass with a giant McDonald's spatula."[185] While the ceremony may have been somewhat unorthodox, the building that would occupy the site of the Stevenson Clinic at 935 East was perfectly in keeping with the character of the Upper East—more so, certainly, than the clinic building itself. Although somewhat larger in scale and distinct in style for the Upper East, the Ronald McDonald House was significant in that, in function, it reinforced the inherently residential nature of the Upper East. It was, after all, a place for people to live. (A second would be added just to the west in 2015.)

The only intrusion into the Upper East's residential environment would appear in 1987 with the construction of medical offices on the former site of the municipal rose garden. It was a fairly undistinguished three-story brick structure with what appears by now to have been the requisite mansard roof. But because it was located in the block occupied by Holy Cross Hospital and Moreau Hall, its function was segregated to a great extent from the rest of the Upper East. That block, in other words, had never been destined to be residential. So the visual and functional impact of this new medical office building was substantially diminished. Had Margaret Lester's imaginary pedestrian wandered east from the Mansion District in, say, 1992, he would have felt very much that he was doing so in 1932.

South Temple's Vanishing Modernism:
"A Fresh Look"

While those lamenting how South Temple has changed have rightfully focused on the loss of some of the jewels of Brigham Street—the Dooly mansion, the Cosgriff mansion, the Judge mansion and others—the impacts of change have not by any means been limited to buildings constructed before 1925. A number of South Temple's signature midcentury buildings have already been demolished, including the Intermountain Clinic Building (South Temple's only building in the Moderne style), the Stevenson Clinic (with its trendy and, for South Temple, rare panelized wall system) and the Beneficial Life Annex (the LDS Church's earliest foray into corporate Modernism).

148

Other significant buildings constructed along South Temple Street between 1925 and 1975 have succumbed not to demolition but to remodeling. Most noteworthy of these is the Kennecott Building, which in 2007 was given a "fresh look."[186] While the building's structure remained intact, the "everlasting metal" was replaced by granite, limestone and glass. The building now bears the name of its (new) primary tenant: Zions Bank. No trace remains that Kennecott Copper or its namesake structure ever occupied the site.

The story of the Kennecott Building is instructive, because it highlights how attitudes about change along South Temple have evolved. While the community in the 1960s and 1970s became increasingly (and justifiably) strident about the loss of Brigham Street's grand estates, it has been noticeably silent

The University Club Building's lower stories took on a completely different appearance in 2016. *Author's collection.*

about the loss of significant buildings from South Temple's midcentury period. Nary a word has been said about the Kennecott Building or the Intermountain Clinic Building or the more recent remodeling of the University Club Building.

Although buildings from the midcentury period may be potentially eligible for listing in the National Register of Historic Places, they generally have not been perceived as "historic" or having meaningful architectural values for South Temple. Salt Lake City's design guidelines for South Temple Street, for example, include no images of buildings constructed during the midcentury period or references to Modernist design ideas, even though a city overview of the South Temple Historic District acknowledges that "these buildings brought a different character to the street and represent a wave of construction that is now appreciated for its mid-twentieth century modern and late modern designs."[187]

Nevertheless, several of the remaining midcentury buildings are now deemed to be historically and/or architecturally significant in their own right. A 2013 survey of the South Temple Historic District identified nine buildings constructed between 1925 and 1975 that are significant: the Manor Apartments, the UEA Building, the Barbara Worth Apartments, the IBM Building, the Metropolitan Life Building, the Masonic temple, the Orthopedic and Fracture Clinic, Moreau Hall and the Mayflower Apartments. Another eight were identified as "contributing" to the character of the historic district. Together, these buildings represent about 15 percent of all the buildings in the South Temple Historic District and, more telling, over 50 percent of the buildings constructed in those blocks between 1925 and 1975.

The recommendations of the 2013 survey clearly indicate that the changes that occurred along Brigham Street did not necessarily, as one walking tour brochure suggests, precipitate "a period of decline from the 1930s through the 1960s."[188] Rather, they introduced a key element to the landscape of South Temple: diversity. While this diversity brought with it certain costs (i.e., the loss of great mansions), it also brought new life, new energy to the street. In the words of Eugene Raskin, "In architecture as in literature and drama, it is the richness of human variation that gives vitality and color to the setting."[189]

More to the point, as painful as the changes along South Temple between 1925 and 1975 may have been for some Salt Lake residents, they were not entirely undesirable. South Temple has always been changing, always been evolving. And that evolution has produced Utah's most architecturally diverse, interesting and significant street.

NOTES

INTRODUCTION

1. Albert F. Phillips, "First Gold Coined in Utah out of Dust Reaching State from California Mill Ditch," *Salt Lake Telegram*, January 2, 1922, http://udn.lib.utah.edu/cdm/compoundobject/collection/tgm30/id/6940/show/7034/rec/1.
2. Lester, *Brigham Street*, 2.
3. Harris and Roberts, "National Register of Historic Places Inventory—Nomination Form," Item 8, 3.
4. Ibid., Item 7, 4.

CHAPTER 1

5. *City Plan*, 28.
6. McCormick, *Gathering Place: An Illustrated History of Salt Lake City*, 64.
7. *City Plan*, 27.
8. Don C. Woodward, "Transport Idea Wins Friends," *Deseret News*, November 8, 1967, https://news.google.com/newspapers?id=E44xAAAAIBAJ&sjid=5kkDAAAAIBAJ&pg=7050,2337366.
9. *Deseret News*, "Right Place for the Auditorium," June 18, 1964, https://news.google.com/newspapers?nid=336&dat=19640618&id=rIwqAAAAIBAJ&sjid=eFgEAAAAIBAJ&pg=5231,4130623&hl=en.
10. Sillitoe, *History of Salt Lake County*, 52.
11. Smith, "National Register of Historic Places Inventory—Nomination Form," Item 8, 1.

12. Max B. Knudson, "Devereaux Gets a New Lease on Life," *Deseret News*, June 3, 1988, https://news.google.com/newspapers?nid=336&dat=198 80603&id=6z5TAAAAIBAJ&sjid=VIQDAAAAIBAJ&pg=7051,733766 &hl=en.

13. Arnold Irvine, "Memories of When Devereaux Was Home," *Deseret News*, n.d.

14. Ibid.

15. *Salt Lake Telegram*, "Interurban Depot Will Be Splendid Structure," January 28, 1923, http://udn.lib.utah.edu/cdm/compoundobject/collection/tgm25/id/110684/show/111012/rec/12.

16. *Ogden Standard*, "Utah Served by Bamberger Co.," January 20, 1927, http://udn.lib.utah.edu/cdm/compoundobject/collection/ogden12/id/55662/show/56206/rec/1.

17. *Salt Lake Telegram*, "Interurban Depot Will Be Splendid Structure," January 28, 1923.

18. Ibid.

19. *Salt Lake Telegram*, "Electric Roads Ready to Start Work on Station," August 21, 1921, http://udn.lib.utah.edu/cdm/compoundobject/collection/tgm6/id/108980/show/109060/rec/1.

20. *Salt Lake Tribune*, "Real Estate Firm in New Quarters," April 6, 1913, http://udn.lib.utah.edu/cdm/compoundobject/collection/sltrib27/id/55526/show/55319/rec/2.

21. *Deseret News*, "Overland Greyhound Bus Station Ceremonies Set," January 11, 1949, https://news.google.com/newspapers?id=1tdjAAAA IBAJ&sjid=ln8DAAAAIBAJ&pg=5261,2299376.

22. *Salt Lake Telegram*, Overland Greyhound Lines advertisement, January 17, 1949, http://udn.lib.utah.edu/cdm/compoundobject/collection/tgm25/id/56160/show/56281/rec/1.

23. *Salt Lake Telegram*, "Police Raid Two Hotels in Clean-Up Drive," December 14, 1928, http://udn.lib.utah.edu/cdm/compoundobject/collection/tgm20/id/50901/show/51057/rec/1.

24. *Salt Lake Telegram*, "Police Crime Raids Continue," March 1, 1935, http://udn.lib.utah.edu/cdm/compoundobject/collection/tgm17/id/127791/show/127913/rec/1.

25. *Salt Lake Tribune*, Lucid Hotel classified advertisement, May 9, 1926, http://newspaperarchive.com/us/utah/salt-lake-city/salt-lake-tribune/1926/05-09/page-38.

26. Downtown Planning Association, "Final Report: Downtown Salt Lake City Second Century Plan," 26.

27. *Deseret News*, "Committee Appointed on Civic Auditorium," May 9, 1934, https://news.google.com/newspapers?nid=336&dat=19340509&id=dJJOAAAAIBAJ&sjid=zrUDAAAAIBAJ&pg=3418,5677645&hl=en.

28. *Deseret News*, "Study the Auditorium," October 14, 1964, https://news.google.com/newspapers?nid=336&dat=19641014&id=iMNNAAAAIBAJ&sjid=jkkDAAAAIBAJ&pg=6700,3041557&hl=en.
29. *Salt Lake Tribune*, "An' Leave the Wrecking to Us," August 17, 1968, http://newspaperarchive.com/us/utah/salt-lake-city/salt-lake-tribune/1968/08-17/pageno-120089327.
30. Arnold Irvine, "Civic Auditorium Rites," *Deseret News*, March 10, 1967, https://news.google.com/newspapers?nid=336&dat=19670310&id=0chOAAAAIBAJ&sjid=Y0kDAAAAIBAJ&pg=7052,2274721&hl=en.
31. ASSIST Incorporated, "West South Temple: A Mixed-Use Development District," Introduction.

CHAPTER 2

32. *Deseret News*, "Dr. Fred Stauffer," October 3, 1903, http://udn.lib.utah.edu/cdm/compoundobject/collection/den3/id/18563/show/18918/rec/4.
33. *Salt Lake Tribune*, "Medical Men Open New Home," February 16, 1927, http://newspaperarchive.com/us/utah/salt-lake-city/salt-lake-tribune/1927/02-16/page-7.
34. Alexander and Allen, *Mormons and Gentiles*, 188.
35. *Salt Lake Telegram*, "Work Soon to Start on Federal Reserve Bank," August 27, 1924, http://udn.lib.utah.edu/cdm/compoundobject/collection/tgm10/id/129406/show/129444/rec/1.
36. *Salt Lake Telegram*, "Modern Buildings Grace Landscape," November 3, 1926, http://udn.lib.utah.edu/cdm/compoundobject/collection/tgm8/id/38437/show/38495/rec/1.
37. *Salt Lake Tribune*, "Big New Hotel for Salt Lake," October 21, 1928, http://newspaperarchive.com/us/utah/salt-lake-city/salt-lake-tribune/1928/10-21/pageno-94801142.
38. *Deseret News*, "Temple Square Hotel Has Anniversary," January 12, 1955, https://news.google.com/newspapers?nid=336&dat=19550112&id=y8BOAAAAIBAJ&sjid=HUoDAAAAIBAJ&pg=4479,2608772&hl=en.
39. *Salt Lake Telegram*, "Our New Underground Garage—Opens June 15th," June 12, 1940, http://udn.lib.utah.edu/cdm/compoundobject/collection/tgm20/id/9581/show/9638/rec/34.
40. *Deseret News*, "Car Parking Crisis Seen for Salt Lake," September 12, 1945, https://news.google.com/newspapers?nid=336&dat=19450912&id=wSVSAAAAIBAJ&sjid=qXcDAAAAIBAJ&pg=4722,1143236&hl=en.

41. *Deseret News and Telegram*, "ZCMI, Contractor Join to Aid Downtown Shoppers," November 1, 1954, https://news.google.com/newspapers?n id=336&dat=19541101&id=-ysKAAAAIBAJ&sjid=u0kDAAAAIBAJ&p g=2737,39046&hl=en.

42. Jack E. Jarrard, "ZCMI Opens 550-Car Park Terrace," *Deseret News/Salt Lake Telegram*, November 2, 1954, https://news.google.com/newspapers? nid=336&dat=19541102&id=f9JOAAAAIBAJ&sjid=u0kDAAAAIBAJ& pg=5895,352319&hl=en.

43. *Salt Lake Tribune*, advertisement for ZCMI parking terrace, October 31, 1954.

44. *City Plan*, 12.

45. Anderson, "Mormon Moderne," 76.

46. *Deseret News*, "New Sharon Building Now Occupied," December 14, 1907, http://udn.lib.utah.edu/cdm/compoundobject/collection/den4/ id/165000/show/165576/rec/1.

47. *Deseret News and Telegram*, "Gone—Forgotten," April 3, 1957, https:// news.google.com/newspapers?nid=336&dat=19570403&id=IEAwAAA AIBAJ&sjid=aUgDAAAAIBAJ&pg=4083,757422&hl=en.

48. *Deseret News and Telegram*, "Beneficial Building Set," April 3, 1957, https://news.google.com/newspapers?nid=336&dat=19570403&id=IE AwAAAAIBAJ&sjid=aUgDAAAAIBAJ&pg=4083,757422&hl=en.

49. Beneficial Financial Group, *A Beneficial Century*, 36.

50. Joseph Lundstrom, "Tower Owners Move into New Offices," *Deseret News*, November 29, 1975, https://news.google.com/newspapers?nid=A ul-kAQHnToC&dat=19751129&printsec=frontpage&hl=en.

51. Hal Knight, "'Civic Heart' Plan Detailed at Meeting on School Sale," *Deseret News/Salt Lake Telegram*, October 8, 1958, https://news.google. com/newspapers?nid=336&dat=19581008&id=42IvAAAAIBAJ&sjid= VUgDAAAAIBAJ&pg=7032,1536189&hl=en.

52. Joseph Lundstrom, "S.L. Landmark Makes Way for Progress," *Deseret News/Salt Lake Telegram*, January 25, 1960, https://news.google.com/ne wspapers?nid=336&dat=19600125&id=LQArAAAAIBAJ&sjid=dUgD AAAAIBAJ&pg=5047,4265544&hl=en.

53. Jack Goodman, "Buildings Reflect Life in Utah over the Past 130-Years Plus," *Salt Lake Tribune*, March 15, 1987.

54. Robert W. Bernick, "ZCMI Schedules New S.L. Store," *Salt Lake Tribune*, April 20, 1961, http://newspaperarchive.com/us/utah/salt-lake-city/ salt-lake-tribune/1961/04-20/pageno-99722193.

55. Robert W. Bernick, "Changes Delay Kennecott Building," *Salt Lake Tribune*, July 7, 1961, http://newspaperarchive.com/us/utah/salt-lake-city/salt-lake-tribune/1961/07-07/page-31.

56. *Kennescope*, "New Quarters for Kennecott," 3.

57. *Kennescope*, "New Home for Kennecott's S.L. Offices," 16.

58. *Salt Lake Tribune*, "Glow of Copper Beautifies Downtown Skyline," November 7, 1965, http://newspaperarchive.com/us/utah/salt-lake-city/salt-lake-tribune/1965/11-07/pageno-93562839.

59. *Kennescope*, "Kennescoops."

60. Jack E. Jarrard, "17-Story Kennecott Building Slated for S.L. Business Area," *Deseret News/Salt Lake Telegram*, May 27, 1959, https://news.google.com/newspapers?nid=336&dat=19590527&id=bUEwAAAAIBAJ&sjid=XkgDAAAAIBAJ&pg=3839,5524422&hl=en.

61. McCormick, *Gathering Place: An Illustrated History of Salt Lake City*, 209.

62. *Deseret News*, "Deseret News Building," March 29, 1902, http://udn.lib.utah.edu/cdm/compoundobject/collection/den7/id/26830/show/27022/rec/4.

63. *Salt Lake Tribune*, photo caption, November 12, 1965, http://newspaperarchive.com/us/utah/salt-lake-city/salt-lake-tribune/1965/11-12/pageno-93562967.

64. Goodman, *As You Pass By*, 41.

65. *Salt Lake Tribune*, photo caption, November 12, 1965, http://newspaperarchive.com/us/utah/salt-lake-city/salt-lake-tribune/1965/11-12/pageno-93562967.

66. *Salt Lake Tribune*, "ZCMI Reports Gains in Sales, Earnings," April 18, 1963, http://newspaperarchive.com/us/utah/salt-lake-city/salt-lake-tribune/1963/04-18/pageno-108848084.

67. *Salt Lake Tribune*, "Changes in Downtown ZCMI," February 20, 1972, http://newspaperarchive.com/us/utah/salt-lake-city/salt-lake-tribune/1972/02-20/pageno-101951478.

68. Ibid.

69. *Salt Lake Tribune*, photo caption, September 21, 1975, http://newspaperarchive.com/us/utah/salt-lake-city/salt-lake-tribune/1975/09-21/pageno-89619688.

70. Goodman, *As You Pass By*, 241.

CHAPTER 3

71. *Salt Lake Herald*, "To Build New Flat," November 2, 1906, http://udn.lib.utah.edu/cdm/compoundobject/collection/slherald5/id/48665/show/48792/rec/2.

72. *Salt Lake Tribune*, ad for the Federal Hotel Apartments, December 19, 1926, http://newspaperarchive.com/us/utah/salt-lake-city/salt-lake-tribune/1926/12-19/pageno-102412840.

73. *Salt Lake Telegram*, "Board Seeks Final Ruling on Zoning," July 2, 1934, http://udn.lib.utah.edu/cdm/compoundobject/collection/tgm17/id/16749/show/16946/rec/1.

74. *Salt Lake Telegram*, "East South Temple Gaining Prestige," November 14, 1926, http://udn.lib.utah.edu/cdm/compoundobject/collection/tgm8/id/42356/show/42426/rec/1.

75. *Salt Lake Telegram*, "A Knotty Problem," February 23, 1935, http://udn.lib.utah.edu/cdm/compoundobject/collection/tgm17/id/135614/show/135713/rec/4.

76. *Salt Lake Telegram*, "South Temple Zoning Measure Is Adopted," May 14, 1935, http://udn.lib.utah.edu/cdm/compoundobject/collection/tgm18/id/11544/show/11726/rec/1.

77. *Salt Lake Telegram*, "Modernism in Decoration of Rooms Prevails," September 26, 1930, http://udn.lib.utah.edu/cdm/compoundobject/collection/tgm16/id/29208/show/29519/rec/7.

78. *Salt Lake Tribune*, ad for the Pasue School, November 17, 1946, http://newspaperarchive.com/us/utah/salt-lake-city/salt-lake-tribune/1946/11-17/pageno-93955844.

79. *Salt Lake Tribune*, "Makoff Cottonwood Mall Fashion Center Opens," March 4, 1964, http://newspaperarchive.com/us/utah/salt-lake-city/salt-lake-tribune/1964/03-04/pageno-91404201.

80. Ibid.

81. *Salt Lake Tribune*, "Makoff to Show Swank Exterior," September 23, 1962, http://newspaperarchive.com/us/utah/salt-lake-city/salt-lake-tribune/1962/09-23/pageno-99713404.

82. *Salt Lake Tribune*, "New Makoff Bonnet Nears Completion," http://newspaperarchive.com/us/utah/salt-lake-city/salt-lake-tribune/1963/03-31/pageno-120078887.

83. Jack Goodman, "The High-Fashion Makoff Store Began Glass-Box Trend," *Salt Lake Tribune*, June 21, 1987.

84. *Salt Lake Tribune*, "Makoff's Starts $1 Million Fashion Center Building," February 27, 1955, http://newspaperarchive.com/us/utah/salt-lake-city/salt-lake-tribune/1955/02-27/pageno-96785928.

85. Robert H. Woody, "'Fifth Avenue' Moving to E. South Temple," *Salt Lake Tribune*, June 29, 1967, http://newspaperarchive.com/us/utah/salt-lake-city/salt-lake-tribune/1967/06-29/pageno-100483590.

86. *Salt Lake Tribune*, "Buys Whitley Home," December 24, 1926, http://newspaperarchive.com/us/utah/salt-lake-city/salt-lake-tribune/1926/12-14/pageno-96007605.

87. *Salt Lake Tribune*, "Cake Baker Gets Tea Room Permit," September 11, 1940, http://newspaperarchive.com/us/utah/salt-lake-city/salt-lake-tribune/1940/09-11/pageno-99457217.

88. Moffitt, *Century of Service*, 123.

89. Utah Education Association House of Delegates Reports, October 9, 1952.

90. James M. Hunter and Associates, "A Regional Office for a National Law Firm," in *Architecture*.

91. *Salt Lake Tribune*, "IBM Branch Moves to New Offices," December 17, 1961, http://newspaperarchive.com/us/utah/salt-lake-city/salt-lake-tribune/1961/12-17/pageno-93745360.

92. Malmquist, *Alta Club*, 77–78.

93. *Salt Lake Tribune*, "Start Nears on Building S.L. 24-Story Structure," November 24, 1963, http://newspaperarchive.com/us/utah/salt-lake-city/salt-lake-tribune/1963/11-24/pageno-108861126.

94. Robert W. Bernick, "Club Will Consider Skyscraper Plan," *Salt Lake Tribune*, April 17, 1963, http://newspaperarchive.com/us/utah/salt-lake-city/salt-lake-tribune/1963/04-17/pageno-108848062.

95. Lester, *Brigham Street*, 77.

96. *Salt Lake Tribune*, ad for Hogle Investment, January 21, 1943, http://newspaperarchive.com/us/utah/salt-lake-city/salt-lake-tribune/1943/01-21/pageno-89924034.

97. *Salt Lake Tribune*, "Formal Reopening Set Today at Brigham Street Pharmacy," June 15, 1949, http://newspaperarchive.com/us/utah/salt-lake-city/salt-lake-tribune/1949/06-15/pageno-120139667.

98. *Salt Lake Tribune*, "LDS Buys Building to House College," June 10, 1961, http://newspaperarchive.com/us/utah/salt-lake-city/salt-lake-tribune/1961/06-10/pageno-93740732.

99. *Deseret News*, "Financing Nearing Completion for New S.L. Office Building," July 15, 1961, https://news.google.com/newspapers?nid=336&dat=19510715&id=LDdPAAAAIBAJ&sjid=jE4DAAAAIBAJ&pg=6813,2850953&hl=en.

100. *Salt Lake Tribune*, "Backers to Present Plans for $8 Million Building," June 3, 1951, http://newspaperarchive.com/us/utah/salt-lake-city/salt-lake-tribune/1951/06-03/pageno-99666747.

101. *Salt Lake Telegram*, "KUTA Purchases Site for Studio," May 4, 1945, http://udn.lib.utah.edu/cdm/compoundobject/collection/tgm23/id/26961/show/27082/rec/1.

102. *Salt Lake Tribune*, "Radio Group Buys New Station Site," May 4, 1945, http://newspaperarchive.com/us/utah/salt-lake-city/salt-lake-tribune/1945/05-04/pageno-90287527.

103. Downtown Planning Association, "Final Report: Second Century Plan."

104. Ibid.

105. Lester, *Brigham Street*, 2.

CHAPTER 4

106. Ibid., 7.

107. Bliss, *Merchants and Miners*, 306.

108. Jones, "Utah Politics 1926–1932," 12.

109. Alexander and Allen, *Mormons and Gentiles*, 133.

110. *Salt Lake Tribune*, ad for Bonneville-on-the-Hill, August 24, 1919. http:// udn.lib.utah.edu/cdm/compoundobject/collection/sltrib32/id/96491/ show/96407/rec/22.

111. *Salt Lake Tribune*, "Old Judge Home Fails to Escape Time and Taxes," July 5, 1933, http://newspaperarchive.com/us/utah/salt-lake-city/salt-lake-tribune/1933/07-05/pageno-99310448.

112. *Deseret News*, "South Temple Is Now to Be Paved," August 25, 1904, http://udn.lib.utah.edu/cdm/compoundobject/collection/den2/ id/100576/show/100744/rec/1.

113. Ibid.

114. *Salt Lake Telegram*, "Resurfacing of Two S.L. Streets Draws Protest," August 16, 1928, http://udn.lib.utah.edu/cdm/compoundobject/ collection/tgm29/id/13918/show/13973/rec/1.

115. *Salt Lake Telegram*, "Auditorium of Masons Will Seat 2000," June 9, 1921, http://udn.lib.utah.edu/cdm/compoundobject/collection/tgm6/ id/86634/show/86869/rec/1.

116. *Deseret News*, "Progress Reported on $500,000 Intermountain Clinic Building in Salt Lake," January 16, 1937, https://news.google.com/new spapers?nid=336&dat=19370116&id=xGg0AAAAIBAJ&sjid=z7UDAA AAIBAJ&pg=5357,1869160&hl=en.

117. Macfarlane, "A History of Inter-Mountain Clinic," 3.

118. *Salt Lake Tribune*, "Medic Center Will Open Late in Fall," September 10, 1950, http://newspaperarchive.com/us/utah/salt-lake-city/salt-lake-tribune/1950/09-10/pageno-94753230.

119. *Salt Lake Tribune*, "Firm Builds New Medical, Dental Office," June 29, 1947, http://newspaperarchive.com/us/utah/salt-lake-city/salt-lake-tribune/1947/06-29/pageno-93964886.

120. *Salt Lake Tribune*, "S.L. Landmark Gives Way to Apartment," January 14, 1946, http://newspaperarchive.com/us/utah/salt-lake-city/salt-lake-tribune/1946/01-14/pageno-91107455.

121. *Salt Lake Tribune*, "Firm Builds New Medical, Dental Office," June 29, 1947.

122. *Salt Lake Tribune*, "Old Houses Hide Behind Modern Fronts," July 21, 1963, http://newspaperarchive.com/us/utah/salt-lake-city/salt-lake-tribune/1963/07-21/pageno-91401104.

123. *Salt Lake Tribune*, "S.L. Landmark to Bow Out," June 21, 1949,

http://newspaperarchive.com/us/utah/salt-lake-city/salt-lake-tribune/1949/06-21/pageno-120139785.

124. Utah State Historic Preservation Office, "Historic Site Form," 2013.

125. *Deseret News*, "Obituary: Richard Russell Steiner," February 3, 2005, http://www.deseretnews.com/article/1310282/Obituary-Richard-Russell-Steiner.html?pg=all.

126. Robert H. Woody, "Center to Replace Cosgriff Mansion," *Salt Lake Tribune*, December 10, 1965, http://newspaperarchive.com/us/salt-lake-city/salt-lake-tribune/1965/12-10/pageno-100474887.

127. Lester, *Brigham Street*, 49.

128. Ibid.

129. Bill Browning, personal interview, September 19, 2013.

130. Ibid.

131. Ibid.

132. Woody, "Center to Replace Cosgriff Mansion."

133. Ann Jardine Bardsley, "The Utah Heritage Foundation Is Dedicated to Preserving Our Past," *Deseret News*, June 21, 1985, https://news.google.com/newspapers?nid=336&dat=19850621&id=zpczAAAAIBAJ&sjid=VYQDAAAAIBAJ&pg=6649,2611713&hl=en.

134. *Salt Lake Tribune*, "Snip of Toweling Signals Opening of New Offices," November 16, 1967, http://newspaperarchive.com/us/utah/salt-lake-city/salt-lake-tribune/1967/11-16/pageno-93733434.

135. Arrington, *From Small Beginnings*, 112.

136. *Salt Lake Tribune*, "Old Judge Home Fails to Escape Time and Taxes," July 5, 1933.

137. Margaret Burton, "Adult Vandalism Decried," *Salt Lake Tribune*, April 19, 1966, http://newspaperarchive.com/us/utah/salt-lake-city/salt-lake-tribune/1966/04-29/pageno-93686666.

138. Suzanne Dean, "Builders Are Looking to the Past," *Deseret News*, November 26, 1974, https://news.google.com/newspapers?nid=Aul-kAQHnToC&dat=19741126&printsec=frontpage&hl=en.

139. *Deseret News*, "Nod for Historic Area," September 26, 1975, https://news.google.com/newspapers?nid=336&dat=19750926&id=HNFSAAAAIBAJ&sjid=IH8DAAAAIBAJ&pg=7055,6525399&hl=en.

140. *Deseret News*, "Demolition Delayed," July 1, 1975, https://news.google.com/newspapers?nid=336&dat=19750701&id=DqQqAAAAIBAJ&sjid=k1sEAAAAIBAJ&pg=5914,205703&hl=en.

141. *Salt Lake Tribune*, "Keyser Buys Terry Home," August 6, 1919, http://udn.lib.utah.edu/cdm/compoundobject/collection/sltrib32/id/37826/show/37806/rec/1.

142. *Salt Lake Telegram*, "Apartment Is Protested," March 15, 1927, http://udn.lib.utah.edu/cdm/compoundobject/collection/tgm28/id/73768/show/73844/rec/1.

CHAPTER 5

143. *Salt Lake Tribune*, "Apartment to Be Last Word in Housing," March 25, 1927, http://newspaperarchive.com/us/utah/salt-lake-city/salt-lake-tribune/1927/03-25/pageno-100902473.

144. Lufkin, "National Register of Historic Places Registration Form: South Temple Historic District Amendment," July 2013.

145. *Salt Lake Tribune*, advertisement for the Mayflower, April 10, 1928, http://newspaperarchive.com/us/utah/salt-lake-city/salt-lake-tribune/1928/04-10/pageno-93971345.

146. *Salt Lake Telegram*, "S.L. Apartment Building Is Sold," December 4, 1936, http://udn.lib.utah.edu/cdm/compoundobject/collection/tgm19/id/45883/show/46093/rec/1.

147. *Deseret News*, "Death: Dorothy Ruth Powell Jensen," July 31, 1991, http://www.deseretnews.com/article/175356.

148. *Salt Lake Tribune*, "Meet Salt Lake's 'Lady Contractor,'" January 20, 1952, http://newspaperarchive.com/us/utah/salt-lake-city/salt-lake-tribune/1952/01-20/pageno-93499291.

149. *Salt Lake Tribune*, "Multi-Unit Construction Moving at Speedy Pace," July 19, 1964, http://newspaperarchive.com/us/utah/salt-lake-city/salt-lake-tribune/1964/07-19/pageno-108857515.

150. William A. Dunn, "Apartment Start Makes Utah Building History," *Deseret News*, June 26, 1964, https://news.google.com/newspapers?nid=336&dat=19640626&id=c8xSAAAAIBAJ&sjid=5n8DAAAAIBAJ&pg=3832,6108275&hl=en.

151. *Salt Lake Tribune*, advertisement for Bonneville Tower, June 5, 1966, http://newspaperarchive.com/us/utah/salt-lake-city/salt-lake-tribune/1966/06-05/pageno-100477207.

152. *Salt Lake Tribune*, "Bank to Manage Apartment House," December 22, 1966, http://newspaperarchive.com/us/utah/salt-lake-city/salt-lake-tribune/1966/12-21/pageno-93723364.

153. *Salt Lake Tribune*, "FHA Forecloses Bonneville Tower, Spacious, $41.2 Million Apartments," December 21, 1966, http://newspaperarchive.com/us/utah/salt-lake-city/salt-lake-tribune/1966/12-21/pageno-93723364.

154. Ibid.

155. *Salt Lake Telegram*, advertisement for "New Modern Apartments," October 19, 1937, http://udn.lib.utah.edu/cdm/compoundobject/collection/tgm34/id/127176/show/127156/rec/2.

156. *Salt Lake Tribune*, "Nurse School Fund Gift Heads Chosen," May 15, 1949, http://newspaperarchive.com/us/utah/salt-lake-city/salt-lake-tribune/1949/05-15/pageno-94777906.

157. *Salt Lake Tribune*, "20 Nurses Last of Long Line," June 14, 1973, http://newspaperarchive.com/us/utah/salt-lake-city/salt-lake-tribune/1973/06-04/pageno-99134807.

158. *Salt Lake Tribune*, "Living Center for Drink Problems Opens in S.L.," February 12, 1974, http://newspaperarchive.com/us/utah/salt-lake-city/salt-lake-tribune/1974/02-12/pageno-89668234.

159. *Deseret News*, "Rose Garden—Time for Uprooting," June 5, 1972, https://news.google.com/newspapers?nid=336&dat=19720605&id=82ZTAAAAIBAJ&sjid=uoUDAAAAIBAJ&pg=6986,952945&hl=en.

160. *Salt Lake Tribune*, "Rose Garden Takes High Spot Among Utah's Scenic Lures," May 21, 1939, http://newspaperarchive.com/us/utah/salt-lake-city/salt-lake-tribune/1939/05-21/pageno-89746889.

161. Burtch Beall, personal interview, March 3, 2015.

162. Hafey, et al, "Historic Preservation: The South Temple Historic District," 3.

163. *Deseret News*, "To Preserve the Past," June 21, 1968, https://news.google.com/newspapers?nid=336&dat=19680621&id=DBMwAAAAIBAJ&sjid=jUoDAAAAIBAJ&pg=3503,4765409&hl=en.

EPILOGUE

164. Ibid.

165. *Deseret News*, "Delta Center Breathes New Life into Area," November 6, 1991, https://news.google.com/newspapers?nid=336&dat=19911106&id=Qd8oAAAAIBAJ&sjid=X4QDAAAAIBAJ&pg=2156,2541442&hl=en

166. Edwards and Daniels Architects, "Holiday Inn Hotel, Salt Lake City, Utah," 1983.

167. Alan Edwards, "Gateway Approval Imminent," *Deseret News*, June 16, 1999, https://news.google.com/newspapers?nid=336&dat=19990616&id=9aJXAAAAIBAJ&sjid=TvMDAAAAIBAJ&pg=1335,80243&hl=en.

168. Ibid.

169. Sherri C. Goodman, "An Update on That Other 'Gateway'…in Salt Lake City," *Deseret News*, February 9, 2003, https://news.google.com/newspapers?nid=894&dat=20030209&id=iZ0_AAAAIBAJ&sjid=ulIDAAAAIBAJ&pg=6641,1340542&hl=en.

170. Tony Semerad, "Slump Deepens at Salt Lake's Gateway Mall," *Salt Lake Tribune*, January 15, 2015, http://www.sltrib.com/news/2063536-155/slump-deepens-at-salt-lake-citys.

171. Max Knudson, "Saudis, Utahns Open Gateway to Future," *Deseret News*, June 1, 1982, https://news.google.com/newspapers?nid=336&dat=19820601&id=sjdTAAAAIBAJ&sjid=HYMDAAAAIBAJ&pg=3182,7679&hl=en.

172. Ibid.

173. Ibid.

174. *Deseret News*, "Khashoggi in Utah: From 1975 to 1986," January 21, 1987, https://news.google.com/newspapers?nid=336&dat=19870121&id=J05TAAAAIBAJ&sjid=64MDAAAAIBAJ&pg=6806,2023789&hl=en.

175. Joseph Linton and Wayne Bingham, "Another Look at the Triad Center Project," *Deseret News*, September 9, 1984, https://news.google.com/newspapers?nid=2318&dat=19840909&id=glgnAAAAIBAJ&sjid=94IDAAAAIBAJ&pg=7217,3526035&hl=en.

176. Max B. Knudson, "Brigham Apartments Replace Eyesore," *Deseret News*, April 9, 1998, https://news.google.com/newspapers?nid=336&dat=19980409&id=ju8jAAAAIBAJ&sjid=k-wDAAAAIBAJ&pg=6751,3989149&hl=en.

177. Glen Warchol, "The Final Confrontation Near on Old Downtown Apartments," *Deseret News*, February 22, 1984, https://news.google.com/newspapers?nid=336&dat=19840222&id=tvRSAAAAIBAJ&sjid=_4IDAAAAIBAJ&pg=6240,3032566&hl=en.

178. *Deseret News*, "Up with the New," February 8, 1986, https://news.google.com/newspapers?nid=336&dat=19860208&id=7tQjAAAAIBAJ&sjid=EoQDAAAAIBAJ&pg=5582,3229153&hl=en.

179. Edwards and Daniels Architects, "Governor's Plaza, Salt Lake City, Utah," undated.

180. *Deseret News*, "Group Opposes U and I Permit," November 4, 1975, https://news.google.com/newspapers?nid=336&dat=19751104&id=iTMpAAAAIBAJ&sjid=7n0DAAAAIBAJ&pg=5457,577298&hl=en.

181. U and I Incorporated, *U and I Incorporated Building*, 1977.

182. *Deseret News*, "Style of the 'Street,'" January 5, 1978, https://news.google.com/newspapers?nid=336&dat=19780125&id=zm1TAAAAIBAJ&sjid=sYUDAAAAIBAJ&pg=6090,5706377&hl=en.

183. *Deseret News*, "Giant Spatula Breaks Ground for Ronald McDonald House," March 15, 1986, https://news.google.com/newspapers?nid=336&dat=19860315&id=pKVhAAAAIBAJ&sjid=NIQDAAAAIBAJ&pg=4104,5718587&hl=en.

184. Brice Wallace, "Zions Tower to Get Fresh Look," *Deseret News*, October 7, 2003, http://www.deseretnews.com/article/515036960/Zions-tower-to-get-fresh-look.html?pg=all.
185. "Design Guidelines for Historic Commercial Properties & Districts in Salt Lake City," 10.
186. Thompson, "Historic South Temple Street Walking Tour," 2.
187. Jacobs, *Death and Life of Great American Cities*, 229.

SELECTED BIBLIOGRAPHY

Alexander, Thomas G. *Grace and Grandeur: A History of Salt Lake City*. Carlsbad, CA: Heritage Media, 2001.

Alexander, Thomas G., and James B. Allen. *Mormons and Gentiles: A History of Salt Lake City*. Boulder, CO: Pruett Publishing, 1984.

Anderson, Charles. *The Growth Pattern of Salt Lake City, Utah, and Its Determining Factors*. Ann Arbor, MI: University Microfilms, 1977.

Anderson, Paul. "Mormon Moderne: Latter-day Saint Architecture 1925–1945." *Journal of Mormon History* 9 (1982): 71–84.

Arrington, Leonard J. *From Small Beginnings: A History of the American Linen Supply Company and Its Successors and Affiliates*. Salt Lake City, UT: Steiner Corporation, c. 1991.

———. *In the Utah Tradition: A History of the Governor's Mansion*. Salt Lake City, UT: Governor's Mansion Foundation, 1987.

Arrington, Leonard J., and Heidi S. Swinson. *The Hotel: Salt Lake's Classy Lady*. Salt Lake City, UT: Publisher's Press, 1986.

ASSIST Incorporated. "West South Temple: A Mixed-Use Development District." Salt Lake City, UT: ASSIST, 1980.

Barnett, Alan. *Seeing Salt Lake City: The Legacy of the Shipler Photographs*. Salt Lake City, UT: Signature Books, 2000.

Beall, Burtch, personal interview, March 3, 2015.

Beneficial Financial Group. *A Beneficial Century: 1905–2005*. Salt Lake City, UT: Beneficial Financial Group, 2005.

Bliss, Jonathan. *Merchants and Miners in Utah: The Walker Brothers and Their Bank*. Salt Lake City, UT: Western Epics, 1983.

SELECTED BIBLIOGRAPHY

Boyce, Ronald R. "An Historical Geography of Greater Salt Lake City Utah." Master's thesis, University of Utah, 1957.

Browning, Bill, personal interview, September 19, 2013.

Burbank, Jeff. *Historic Photos of Salt Lake City*. Nashville, TN: Turner Publishing, 2008.

———. *Remembering Salt Lake City*. Nashville, TN: Turner Publishing, 2010.

Carman, Frank, interview by Tim Larson, 1986. Interview 162, transcript, Everett Cooley Oral History Project, J. Willard Marriott Library Special Collections, University of Utah, Salt Lake City.

Carter, Thomas, and Peter Goss. *Utah's Historic Architecture, 1847–1940*. Salt Lake City: Utah State Historical Society, 1988.

City Plan: Salt Lake City, Utah. Salt Lake City, UT: Salt Lake City Corporation, 1943.

Curtis, William J.R. *Modern Architecture Since 1900*. 3rd ed. London: Phaidon Press, 1996.

Deseret Book: Commemorating 110 Years of Service. Salt Lake City, UT: Deseret Book, 1976.

"Design Guidelines for Historic Commercial Properties & Districts in Salt Lake City." Salt Lake City, UT: Salt Lake City, undated. Part III, 10.

Downtown Planning Association. "Final Report: Downtown Salt Lake City Second Century Plan." Salt Lake City: Utah Chapter American Institute of Architects, 1962.

Edwards and Daniels Architects. "Governor's Plaza, Salt Lake City, Utah." N.d.

———. "Holiday Inn Hotel, Salt Lake City, Utah." 1983.

Egleston, Elizabeth. "For Commerce, Copper, and Children: The Architecture of Scott & Welch, 1914–38." *Utah Historical Quarterly* 59 (Spring 1991): 104–22.

Emerson, Peter DuPont. "The South Temple Historic District: Past, Present, Future." Master's thesis. University of Utah Graduate School of Architecture, 1979.

The Encyclopedia of Utah. St. Clair Shores, MI: Somerset Publishers, 2001.

Federal Writers' Project. *Utah: A Guide to the State*. New York: Hastings House, 1945.

Fohlin, E.V. *Salt Lake City Past and Present*. Salt Lake City, UT: Skelton Publishing, 1908.

Gelernter, Mark. *A History of American Architecture: Buildings in Their Cultural and Technological Context*. Hanover, NH: University Press of New England, 1999.

Goodman, Jack. *As You Pass By: Architectural Musings on Salt Lake City*. Salt Lake City: University of Utah Press, 1995.

Goss, Peter L., and Charles Hughes. "Historical Report: South Temple Improvements." March 4, 1998.

"Greater Salt Lake City Land Usage." Salt Lake City: Salt Lake County Planning Commission, 1955.

Hafey, Mark, et al. "Historic Preservation: The South Temple Historic District." Salt Lake City, 1975.

Harris, Lois, and Allen Roberts. "National Register of Historic Places Inventory—Nomination Form." Salt Lake City, 1978.

"Historic American Buildings Survey: Devereaux (Staines-Jennings Mansion)." Salt Lake City, 1967.

"Historic Buildings Along South Temple Street." Salt Lake City: Utah Heritage Foundation, 1980.

"Historic Sites Survey: Devereaux." Salt Lake City, 1969.

Hitchcock, Henry Russell, and Philip Johnson. *The International Style*. New York: W.W. Norton & Company, 1995.

Huffaker, Kirk. *Salt Lake City Then and Now*. San Diego, CA: Thunder Bay Press, 2007.

Jackson, Richard. *Places of Worship: 150 Years of Latter-day Saint Architecture*. Provo, UT: Religious Studies Center, Brigham Young University, 2003.

Jacobs, Jane. *The Death and Life of Great American Cities*. New York: Vintage Books, 1992.

James M. Hunter and Associates. *Architecture*. "A Regional Office for a National Law Firm." Boulder, CO: James M. Hunter and Associates, n.d.

Jones, Dan E. "Utah Politics 1926–1932." PhD diss., University of Utah, 1968.

Kennescope. "Kennescoops" (October 1959).

———. "New Home for Kennecott's S.L. Offices" (November–December 1965).

———. "New Quarters for Kennecott" (May–June 1965).

Lester, Margaret. *Brigham Street*. Salt Lake City: Utah State Historical Society, 1979.

Lufkin, Beatrice. "National Register of Historic Places Registration Form: South Temple Historic District Amendment." Salt Lake City, 2013.

Macfarlane, Allen P. "A History of Inter-Mountain Clinic." Unpublished manuscript, March 1992.

Malmgren, Larry H. "A History of the WPA in Utah." Master's thesis, Utah State University, 1965.

Malmquist, O.N. *The Alta Club 1883–1974*. Salt Lake City, UT: Alta Club, 1974.

May, Dean L. *Utah: A People's History*. Salt Lake City: University of Utah Press, 1987.

McCormick, John S. *The Gathering Place: An Illustrated History of Salt Lake City*. Salt Lake City, UT: Signature Books, 2000.

———. *The Historic Buildings of Downtown Salt Lake City*. Salt Lake City: Utah State Historical Society, 1982.

McCormick, John S., and Diana Johnson. "Salt Lake City Business District Multiple Resource Area (Partial Inventory: Historic and Architectural Properties)." September 1981.

Moffitt, John Clifton. *A Century of Service*. Salt Lake City: Utah Education Association, 1961.

Murphy, Miriam B. "Simon Bamberger." Accessed October 27, 2013. http://historytogo.utah.gov/people/simonbamberger.html.

National Bureau of Economic Research. "Railroad Revenue, Passenger Miles, Total for United States." Retrieved from Federal Reserve Bank of St. Louis. https://fred.stlouisfed.org/series/M03010USM429NNBR.

Peter, John. *Masters of Modern Architecture*. New York: Bonanza Books, 1958.

"A Report of Land Use in Salt Lake City." Salt Lake City, UT: Salt Lake City Planning Commission; Salt Lake City Community Improvement Program, 1972.

Roberts, Allen D. "Religious Architecture of the LDS Church: Influence and Changes Since 1847." *Utah Historical Quarterly* 43 (1975): 327.

———. *Salt Lake City's Historic Architecture*. Charleston, SC: Arcadia Publishing, 2012.

———. "A Survey of LDS Architecture in Utah: 1847–1930." Unpublished manuscript, last modified 1974.

Roper, Roger. "Housemakers in Transition: Women in Salt Lake City Apartments, 1910–1940." *Utah Historical Quarterly* 67, no. 4 (Fall 1999).

Safeway. "Our Story." http://www.safeway.com/ShopStores/Our-Story.page.

Salt Lake City Board of Adjustment Case Files, various.

Salt Lake City Demolition Permit Records, 1914–1976.

Salt Lake City Directory. New York: R.L. Polk & Company, various years.

"Salt Lake City Zoning Ordinance 1974." Salt Lake City, UT: Salt Lake City Planning Commission, 1974.

Salt Lake County Abstracts, Salt Lake County Recorder, various.

Sanborn Fire Insurance Maps. New York: Sanborn Map Company, various.

"Scott, Louie & Browning, Architects and Engineers." Salt Lake City, UT: Scott, Louie & Browning, n.d.

Sillitoe, Linda. *A History of Salt Lake County*. Salt Lake City: Utah Historical Society, Salt Lake County Commission, 1996.

Smith, Melvin T. "National Register of Historic Places Inventory—Nomination Form." Salt Lake City: Utah Historical Society, Item 8, 1, 1970.

Swett, Ira L. *Interurbans of Utah*. Cerritos, CA: Interurbans, 1974.

Taylor, Samuel W. *Rocky Mountain Empire: The Latter-day Saints Today*. New York: Macmillan, 1978.

Thompson, Lisa. "Historic South Temple Street Walking Tour." Salt Lake City: Utah Heritage Foundation, 2001.

"Time Travel on South Temple." Salt Lake City: Utah Heritage Foundation, c. 2001.

U and I Incorporated. *U and I Incorporated Building: A New Landmark on South Temple in Salt Lake City*. 1977.

U.S. Internal Revenue Service. "Statistics of Income." Various.

Utah Education Association House of Delegates Reports, October 9, 1952.

Utah History Encyclopedia. "Kennecott Corporation." http://www.uen.org/utah_history_encyclopedia/k/KENNECOTT_CORPORATION.html.

UtahRails.net. "Union Pacific Buses." http://utahrails.net/up/union-pacific-buses.php.

Utah State Historic Preservation Office. "Historic Site Form." 2013.

Westwood, Frances Jean. Interview by Gregory Thompson and Floyd O'Neil, 1987. Interview 448, transcript, Everett Cooley Oral History Project, J. Willard Marriott Library, Salt Lake City.

Westwood, Jean Miles. *Madame Chair: The Political Autobiography of an Unintentional Pioneer*. Logan: Utah State University Press, 2007.

Westwood, Richard E. *Dreams Can Come True: An Autobiography*. Salt Lake City: Utah State Historical Society, 1997.

"The Winning of Barbara Worth." Accessed July 2, 2014. http://www.amazon.com/Winning-Barbara-Worth-Harold-Wright/dp/1565544722.

Wiseman, Carter. *Twentieth Century American Architecture: The Buildings and Their Makers*. New York: W.W. Norton, 2000.

"Zoning Map of Salt Lake City." Salt Lake City: Salt Lake City Engineering Department, c. 1940.

INDEX

INDEX

Index

ABOUT THE AUTHOR

Bim Oliver is a consultant specializing in Utah architecture of the twentieth century. He lives in Salt Lake City with his spouse, Cyndy, their dog, Sam, and cat, Max.